William's War

by

Priscilla Winn.

Grosvenor House
Publishing Limited

This book is published by
Grosvenor House Publishing Ltd
28-30 High Street, Guildford, Surrey, GU1 3HY.
www.grosvenorhousepublishing.co.uk

"William's War" is a fictional story based on events in history. Any resem-
blance to persons living or dead is purely coincidental.

A CIP record for this book
is available from the British Library

ISBN 1-905529-51-1

For my grandsons
Aaron Hopkins and Clinton Farmer
With much love.

Petts Wood
Kent
1944

1 "William. William!" The sirens are sounding. It's time to get into the air raid shelter"

My Mother's voice wakes me from a deep sleep and I struggle to keep my eyes open. I've been having a lovely dream. In the dream, I was at the seaside, and I had rowed a small boat across the water to an island, that I'd noticed lying a short distance off the coast. The dream was just getting to the interesting bit. I was climbing out of the boat and pulling it onto the shingle beach. Perhaps I would meet fierce pirates or maybe find boxes of buried treasure. I don't want to wake up.

"Come on William!"

My head feels really dizzy and it's hard to keep myself fully awake. It's been the same for the past three nights – sirens sounding not long after we have got settled into bed. I'm so tired. All that I want to do is to sleep.

"Don't forget your gas mask and do hurry up!" calls Mother.

I drag myself out of my warm bed, search in the dark for my dressing gown and stub my big toe painfully on the hearth of the fireplace. When I've found the dressing gown, I take out the tiny torch, which I keep in one of the pockets. Even though we have blackout curtains up at all the windows, my parents won't let me turn on the bedroom light when there is an air raid, but the torch is ok because it gives out only a small beam. The German pilots would never be able to see such a faint light, but they can see lights from houses, so that's why we have the blackout. Mother is a part time Air Raid Patrol Warden and when she is on duty, she has to make sure that no lights are showing from windows. People can get fined for not blacking out their houses properly.

The gas mask is hanging from the arm of a chair. I hate the thing. In the torchlight it looks like a monster's head with two great round holes where its eyes should be. We have to take our gas masks with us everywhere we go in case of a gas attack. There hasn't been one yet, but some people who remember the First World War, think that the Germans may very likely drop gas onto us from planes. What worries me is, if this happens, how can I protect Tilly?

I grab the mask and bend down to pick up Tilly. She's sleepy too and probably doesn't want to leave her cosy basket with the woolly blanket that Mrs Thomas from next door helped me to knit out of scraps of wool left over from some of her husband's jumpers, which she unpicked. Like most things, wool is in short supply. Mrs Thomas knits any wool she can get hold of into socks to send out to the soldiers who are fighting for us. I'm not much good at knitting – you can see which bits of the blanket that are my work, but although there are a few holes where I dropped some stitches, that's not likely to bother Tilly. Joe, a boy in my class at school, saw me knitting. He went and told all the other boys. Now, some of them call me a sissy.

Tilly has been with us for about two months. It was strange, the way she came into our lives. She just arrived one morning out of nowhere, walking in through the kitchen door, covered in dust and soot and looking an awful mess. Mother reckoned that she might have come from a bombed house. There had been an air raid the night before and some houses a few streets away had been hit. We set about cleaning her up. Instead of being a completely black cat as first we thought, we discovered that she had four white feet, a white tip on her tail and a little white face. She was tiny compared to some of the cats that I'd seen. I don't know why I named her Tilly. The name just came into my head, but it seemed to suit her.

Tilly was very friendly in spite of the ordeal, which she must have suffered. She was also very hungry. There wasn't much food to spare because now there is a war, our food is rationed, but we managed to find a few scraps and gave her a saucer of milk.

Mother said that we must put a sign on the front gate to say that we had found a cat, in case Tilly's owners came looking for her. We did this, but no one claimed her.

Tilly seems to like living with us and she has become one of the family. There's only Mother, Father and myself and I get a bit lonely at times, so it's nice to have a pet to look after. Father isn't too keen on cats, but I know that Mother loves Tilly and it was she who persuaded Father to let us keep our little stray.

With Tilly under my right arm and the gas mask in my left hand, I hurry down the stairs, guided by the torch that Father is shining for me to find my way.

"I don't know why you bring that cat with you. The Government reckons that it is better to let cats go off on their own. They are supposed to be good at looking after themselves" he says.

"Oh Harold, let William bring Tilly with him if he wants to" Mother has just arrived at the foot of the stairs.

"Alright. Come along now and put those gas masks on before we go outside"

We put on the masks, go out the back door and down the garden, to the sound of sirens wailing. I hold my hand over Tilly's nose, in case there is gas in the air.

Scrambling into the shelter, we remove the masks and sit on the beds. We have three wooden bunks that aren't very comfortable. Mother and I can stand up in the shelter, but Father, who is a little taller than the six feet height of the shelter, has to be careful not to bump his head. There's an earth floor, which always seems to be damp because every time that it rains the place gets flooded. Mother says the damp soil is good for the mushrooms and rhubarb, which she grows in a small corner of the shelter. When the war started, she dug up all her beautiful rose bushes and lawn to turn the garden into a vegetable patch. We were told that farmers couldn't grow enough vegetables. Instead, they had to grow fodder to feed the cattle because the war stopped the import of cattle feed from other countries. Everyone got leaflets about how to grow their own food.

"Dig for Victory" we were told.

Mother has grown some lovely vegetables and I try to help her whenever I can. I grow mustard and cress on blotting paper in my bedroom. It tastes quite nice in sandwiches.

Some people keep chickens and there are pig clubs where pigs are raised for meat. We give all our vegetable peelings to Mr Parker who keeps chickens. Nothing is wasted. I remember, when I was about six years old, going to see a man called Mr Jones, to take some peelings for his pig. I liked Fred, as the pig was named. Fred made funny little grunting noises and he would let me scratch his bristly head. I used to think that he was just a pet. When I found out that poor Fred was going to be eaten one day, it really upset me.

We have a box full of clothes in the shelter, and because we are in our nightwear and there wasn't time to dress properly, Mother finds some thick jumpers to put on over our pyjamas.

I feel a bit warmer in the woolly jumper, and with Tilly lying beside me, I wrap myself up in the blankets on the bunk bed. Tilly is being very good about having to be dragged down the garden in the middle of the night and the noise outside doesn't seem to bother her much. She must be getting used to it. But I know that I will never get used to it. I want to pull the blankets over my head and blot out the sounds, but I can't. I'm frightened and I have to listen. We are supposed to be safer in air raid shelters than in our houses, but I wonder as I do every time that we come in here, if a bomb will fall and kill us all.

The shelters were brought to us on the back of lorries in 1940. There were six curved corrugated iron sheets and two end pieces, one for the front and one for the back of the shelter. I tried to help my parents dig the three feet deep pit that had to be ten foot long and four foot wide. It was dry weather and it took ages to do the digging. I remember that I got blisters on my hands from holding the spade. After we had finished the pit, Father bolted the iron sheets together to assemble the shelter in the pit. Then, all the earth from the pit had to be used to cover the shelter. It was exhausting work.

Mother found an old tin of paint and painted the inside of the shelter white. She even stuck a couple of pretty pictures on the walls. Father said what was the point of doing this, but Mother just said if a jobs worth doing, it's worth doing properly and didn't he agree that it looked a bit more cheery now?

Even though I feel so tired, I find it difficult to get to sleep in the shelter. It's like being in a tin can, and it's so noisy when there is a raid going on. Father says that the corrugated iron walls make the sounds even louder. Some people spend every night in their shelters; others have got so fed up with them that they don't bother to use them any more. We go in ours only when there is an air raid warning.

Suddenly, there is a very loud blast, which is almost deafening. The shelter's tin walls rattle, and we know that a bomb must have fallen nearby. In the leaflet that we got when the shelter was delivered, it said that the Anderson shelter as it is known, can withstand almost anything but a direct hit, but I have heard that some shelters collapsed when bombs fell close to them.

London is the main target for the German bombers, but here, on the outskirts in Petts Wood, we still get bombs dropping and Kent is being called "Doodlebug Alley" after the V1 bombers, which are small pilotless planes that fall to earth and explode when they run out of fuel. Anti air- craft defences try to shoot down the doodlebugs before they reach London.

We hear more explosions that sound further away and then the noises stop.

I must have eventually got off to sleep, because the next thing that I know is that it is morning and the "All Clear" siren is sounding. It's safe to come out of the shelter.

Mother, Father and I crawl out of the shelter and look to see if our house is still standing. It seems ok, as do the houses on either side of us. Mrs Thomas calls to Mother over the garden fence.

"What a night! I was in the bath when those sirens went off. I'm trying to do my bit as the Government asks, bathing only once a week in no more than five inches of warm water because of the coal shortage, so I thought blow it! I'm not getting out of this bath for anyone! Those Germans have got no respect. Can't even have a bath in peace to make myself beautiful for my Stan"

I try not to laugh at what Mrs Thomas has just said. She's 65 if she's a day, and I can't imagine her and her husband Stan all lovey dovey.

We go into the kitchen to find broken crockery and plaster dust all over the place. Mother's best china plates have been blown off the dresser and bits of the ceiling have come down. The ceiling in the bathroom, which is above the kitchen, has also got damage, but the other rooms are alright, apart from a few broken ornaments.

Tilly is meowing for food, but Mother says that she will have to wait until we have tidied up the mess. Father says that he will go and see if he can be of some help to any neighbours that may not have got off as lightly as we have. He tells me to stay and help Mother.

It takes quite a while to clear up the mess. Thankfully, the water is still on so we can wash the floor after sweeping up the broken china and plaster. Sometimes, a main water pipe gets hit and we are without water in the house until the pipe is mended.

Father comes back and says that two houses in our road have been almost demolished by a bomb. The people who live there were in their air raid shelters when the bomb landed, so miraculously they escaped unhurt, but they are very shaken and have lost most of their belongings. Everyone is rallying round to help them salvage anything worth saving.

Today is a school day, so after breakfast, I collect my satchel and set off to my school which is only about ten minutes walk away. I have to pass the bombed houses. It's really bad, such a mess. The houses don't look much like houses anymore, just a mixture of rubble and broken furniture. A few pieces of furniture, which have survived the bombing, are stacked on the pavement.

An old lady is sitting on a chair crying softly. I don't know her name, but I see her sometimes working in her garden when I walk by on my way home from school. Once, she gave me a piece of cake. I feel really sorry for her, and I reach into my pocket for the last jellybaby from my sweet ration. These are my favourite sweets, but I think that the old lady needs it more than I do.

"Please stop crying" I say, taking her hand and placing the jellybaby in it.

She looks at the jellybaby then up at me. Wiping her eyes on her apron, she says

"Thank you lad. I haven't had one of these for ages. It's good that it's a soft sweet. I was in such a rush to get into the air raid shelter, that I left my false teeth in the glass beside my bed" She smiles at me with a toothless grin.

2 When I get to school, there are men taking down the iron railings from the playground and loading them onto a lorry. All the railings from the parks around here have already been removed and now schools and houses with railings are being stripped to supply metal to make weapons.

There was an appeal for aluminium pots, pans and saucepans to make into planes. 5,000 pans were needed to make a fighter plane and 25,000 to make a bomber. Mother had a couple of old saucepans, which she gave up. We live only a few miles from Biggin Hill air station and every time that I see one of our planes flying overhead, I wonder if it's the one made from mother's saucepans.

There are posters up asking us to have "Salvage Drives" to collect bottles, rags, scrap metal and bones. The paper that the posters are printed on is also in short supply, so we save every piece we get to give to be recycled. I gave up all my old comics plus my "Treasure Island" book. Mother said that I didn't need to give my favourite book away, but I really wanted to help and anyway, I know the story so well, that it's all in my mind.

Most of the children are talking about last night's air raid. At break time, in the playground, the boys play games about the war. I never join in – it doesn't seem right somehow. There are a few empty desks in our classroom. Some of the children have gone to stay in the country away from the bombing, evacuees they are called. My best friend James has gone to Wales to his Gran's house and I miss him a lot.

After school, I decide to walk home a different way, by cutting across the recreation ground. I've just reached the alleyway that leads from the recreation ground to the housing estate, when I notice Joe and three other boys halfway down the alley leaning against the wooden fence.

They see me and start whispering together. Then, Joe calls out "Hello sissy. Where's your knitting?" I try to ignore him and keep walking. I don't want to turn around and walk back. That would just show that I'm frightened of them.

The boys stand across the path, blocking my way.

"Cos you know why he's a sissy don't you" Joe is talking again.

"No why?" says one of the other boys.

"Well, his dads a conchie"

"What's that" asks another of the boys.

"A conscientious objector. Our dads all signed up, and risk their lives to protect us, whilst his dad stays at home and refuses to fight. Stands to reason, with a dad like that, he couldn't be anything else but a sissy" Joe sniggers at me.

"Let me pass please" I say, but they don't move and start chanting "sissy" and "conchie"

They have no intention of letting me pass, so to avoid trouble, I turn around intent on going back the way I have just come. Suddenly, Joe grabs my arm and pulls me back. He's bigger and stronger than I am and although I try to push him away, he pins me against the fence. One of the other boys, snatches my satchel, undoes it and empties everything onto the path.

"Can't find any knitting. He must have left it at home" he says.

"Perhaps his dad's doing some for him" says Joe and they all laugh.

They stamp on my books and pencils with their muddy feet. I bend down and try to pick up my things but they push me onto the ground. The path is covered with broken glass, which has probably come from the blown out windows of a nearby house that was bombed. I feel the glass biting into my knees and the palms of my hands. It really hurts, but I'm determined not to let them see my pain.

I struggle to pull a handkerchief out of my pocket to wipe my bleeding hands. The boys keep kicking my belongings along the path, then they seem to get bored with tormenting me and run off across the recreation ground.

I stand up and dab my knees with the handkerchief. One knee isn't too bad but the other has a deep cut, which won't stop bleeding. I tie the handkerchief around my knee, then start to pick up my books. The books are covered in mud and most of my pencils are broken.

Why did they pick on me? I've never given them any bother. Is my Father a conscientious objector? I know that most of the boys in my class have Fathers in the National Service, or if they aren't serving they are in reserved occupations.

I must admit that I have sometimes wondered why my Father hasn't joined up. I suppose that I thought that it was because he was too old. My parents are a few years older than the other children's parents. When the war started, men between the ages of eighteen and forty one were likely to be called upon to serve their country. At first only the younger men were called up, but by1941, older men were needed too. I do a quick bit of mental arithmetic. I think that my Father was born in 1903, so he would have been thirty eight years old in 1941. He wasn't too old to join the war.

I can understand why some men don't want to fight. War is an awful thing and no one wants to kill another human being. I can also understand why people dislike conscientious objectors. They must feel that these men are not doing their bit to help bring an end to the terrible situation that we are living through.

I decide to try to find out why Father hasn't joined the war. I can't just ask him, but perhaps I might be able to mention it to Mother. I don't want to upset them and I'm sure that whatever reasons my Father has for not joining up, they are good ones.

Father certainly isn't a coward. He was one of the first part time volunteers to join the Auxiliary Fire Service, which was set up when the regular fire service couldn't cope with all the fires that started after the bombs fell.

As I turn into my road, I hope that Mother is out and that I might be able to clean myself without her having to see the mess I'm in. But, when I open the kitchen door, she is there making "Woolton Pie" This vegetable pie is named after Lord Woolton, the Minister of Food. You use whatever vegetables that are in season, thicken them with oatmeal and cover the mixture with potato pastry or mashed potato topped with cheese if you can get any. It tastes quite nice.

Mother looks up from what she is doing and immediately notices the state of me.

"William, whatever has happened to you?" she asks.

"I fell over on the path from the recreation ground and cut myself on some broken glass" I'm not going to tell her about Joe and the boys.

"Well, you had better let me take a look at those cuts. They seem rather nasty" She leaves the pie and goes off to the bathroom to collect the first aid box.

When she comes back, she fills a basin with warm water, pulls out a chair from the kitchen table and tells me to sit down.

After washing and drying my hands, Mother dabs the cuts with iodine and puts plasters over them. Then she cleans my left knee and puts iodine on that too. The handkerchief that I tied around my right knee is covered in blood and when she unties it, my knee is still bleeding.

When Mother tries to clean the cut, a pain shoots up my leg.

"Ouch, that hurts" I say.

Mother looks closely at the cut and finds a piece of glass stuck in it.

"I'll have to get this out. It might hurt a bit, but I'll be as gentle as possible" she says.

I flinch as the glass is removed.

"The cut isn't very long but it is quite deep where the glass went in. I don't think that it will need stitching, but it will need a bandage on it for a while. You've really been in the wars" she says, then laughs at the expression that she has just used.

Whilst Mother is cooking the Woolton Pie, I go up to my bedroom and take my books out of my satchel. I don't know what my teacher will say when she sees the mess the books are in. All the brown paper covers are dirty with mud and there are footprints from Joe and his friends' shoes. I haven't got any more paper to recover the books. Like I said, paper is in short supply.

With a clean handkerchief, I rub off the worst of the mud, but the books still look awful. Then, I have an idea. What if I paint over the covers. I don't have much paint left in my paint box, so I get a sponge and dip it in the darker colours, then I dab the sponge on the book covers. This gives quite a good mottled effect and more importantly, it hides the footprints. I write some labels with my name and the subject on them, and after sticking these on the books, I'm quite pleased with the end result. I even manage to find a couple of pencils in a drawer to replace the broken ones.

Mother calls up to tell me that dinner is ready, and I realise how hungry I am when I smell the cooked pie. I give Tilly her tea, which she eats very quickly, then meows for more. She seems to be even more hungry than usual lately and I try to sneak bits of my meal for her, but with so little food to go round, it isn't easy. If Father caught me giving some of my meat ration to Tilly, he would be very cross.

The pie is lovely and then we have National Loaf with jam. The jam tastes nice, but the loaf is dry and coarse, not like the bread we used to have. White flour is impossible to get now, so this bread is made by using nearly all of the wheat including the husk, and its got added calcium. It looks a dirty beige colour. The Ministry of Food says it's good for us, but most people think that it tastes horrible.

Tilly's not too pleased because I haven't been able to give her some meat. There wasn't any in our meal tonight. I offer to do the washing up and when Mother and Father have gone into the sitting room and I'm alone in the kitchen, I mix up a little dried milk and water to give to Tilly.

I've finished the washing up. Mother suggests that we play a game of Monopoly. I love this game and hope that we won't be interrupted by another air raid. This often happens. It's very annoying.

No sirens sound, so we carry on playing Monopoly until my bedtime. Tilly follows me upstairs and settles into her basket. She rubs her face on her blanket, yawns and then closes her eyes. I have a quick wash, clean my teeth and get into bed.

"Goodnight Tilly" I say.

Well, it's morning and I'm still in my bed. I suppose that there wasn't an air raid last night or Mother would have come to wake me. Time to get up for breakfast.

3

I get dressed and then check that I've packed all the books I need for school today. I don't know what Miss Adams will say about the book covers. I have to hand in two of the books that have homework due in today.

Downstairs, Mother is making breakfast and listening to her favourite programme "The Kitchen Front" which is on nearly every morning. She writes down any recipes that sound worth trying. Father has already gone to work, so I might get time to ask her about why he hasn't joined up.

"How's your knee this morning William?" she asks.

"Not too bad. My hands feel a bit sore"

"I'll have a look at them after breakfast. There should be time before you go off to school" she says.

Usually, for breakfast we have National Loaf toasted.

What a surprise when Mother puts a plate with toast and a boiled egg in front of me! I can't believe what I'm seeing. The shortage of eggs is really bad. You don't get weekly or monthly rations of them as you do with other foods. Eggs are available only when there are enough to go round. I haven't had a fresh egg for ages. There are dried eggs, which come in tins or packets and we get these every two months, but they're not the same as fresh eggs.

14

"Mr Parker's hens have started laying again and he brought round an egg for each of us to say thank you for all the vegetable peelings we give him to mix with the chicken meal" she says.

It's lovely, dipping the toast into the golden egg yolk and all too soon, the egg is gone. I would love another, but I'm lucky to have had even one fresh egg. I hope Mr Parker's hens keep on laying and that he gives us more eggs when he can spare them.

I was going to ask Mother about Father not joining the war, but there isn't much time before I have to leave for school. She gets the first aid box and starts to unwind the bandage on my knee. The last bit of bandage has stuck to my knee and it's all weepy. Mother puts some ointment on the cut and then ties another bandage over it. My hands hurt more than my knee does. It's difficult to rest them. After taking off the plasters and putting on ointment and new plasters, Mother says

"I'm afraid that your hands may be sore for a while, but everything seems to be healing nicely. Your knee is much better so try not to knock it while you are at school, then the bandage will be able to come off soon."

Tilly arrives through the kitchen door, carrying a dead mouse in her mouth. Mother shoos her out of the kitchen and she goes a few yards along the garden path, then sits down and starts to eat her prize. I know that it's in a cat's nature to catch mice, but I still feel sorry for the little mouse.

Miss Adams is in a good mood. She isn't popular with all the children in the class, but I quite like her. She is fairly strict, and even Joe, who mucks around whenever he can get the chance with some of our other teachers, behaves well when he is in Miss Adams's lessons.

Halfway through the lesson, Miss Adams tells us to bring our homework books up to her desk.

"You're for it now" Joe says and smirks at me.

Unfortunately, his desk is opposite mine.

I get the book out of my satchel and wait until some of the other children start to go up to Miss Adams's desk with their books. Miss Adams is writing something on the blackboard, but unluckily for me, she turns round just as I am placing my book on top of the others.

"William, what have you done to your book?" she asks as she notices the cover.

"Sorry Miss. I tripped over yesterday and my books fell out of my satchel into some mud. I couldn't re-cover them as I didn't have any paper because of the shortage, so I cleaned the covers the best I could and dabbed paint on them to try to make them look better."

"Well" she says, picking up my book and looking at it closely "You haven't done a bad job and you have shown initiative. Well done"

Miss Adams often uses words that I don't understand. I don't know what initiative means, but she seems to be pleased with me. I'll look up the word in the dictionary when I get home.

Miss Adams returns to the blackboard and I take the chance to poke my tongue out at Joe, who looks quite upset that I haven't been punished.

I decide to take the usual route home from school, keeping away from the alley where Joe may be waiting to have another go at me.

Tilly greets me as I open the front gate. She purrs loudly when I stroke her back and rubs her side against my leg. Then, she runs along beside me as I go round the back of the house to the kitchen door.

"Did you have a good day at school William?" Mother asks.

She is mending some of our clothes. Before the war, we could afford new ones when the old ones began to wear out, but now because lots of the factories that used to make clothes have stopped doing so and instead make things needed for the war, clothes are in short supply. You get coupons to exchange for what there is available. This year, it's 48 coupons for each person. The coupons don't go very far, so we have to be careful with everything we wear and make clothes last as long as possible. As I'm still growing and need bigger clothes every so often, Mother goes to the Women's Voluntary Service Clothing Exchange and hands in the clothes I've grown out of in exchange for bigger ones. She comes home with some odd things sometimes, but I can't be fussy.

Mother was never interested in dressmaking before the war. Now, she's quite good at it. When her dressing gown fell to pieces, she made another one out of an old candlewick bedspread.

"Yes, it was good today" I reply.

I remember Miss Adams's word – initiative. I go into the sitting room and take the dictionary out of the bookcase. But, I don't know how to spell initiative.

"Mother. How do you spell initiative?" I call from across the hall.

"INITIATIVE" she replies.

Thanking her, I look up the word.

It says

"A new action or movement, often intended to solve a problem"

Well, I think that we all need plenty of initiative to get through this war.

4

Mother is on Air Raid Patrol duty this evening. She goes off wearing her blue uniform and tin hat with W for warden painted on it.

Apart from checking that the houses are blacked out properly, she also has to help deal with any small fires that might start, take people whose houses get bombed to rest centres and carry out first aid.

She told me that at the beginning of the war in 1939, the black-out caused lots of accidents. In the darkness people were killed and injured when they got hit by cars, fell down steps and kerb stones, walked into trees, walls, telephone boxes and pillar boxes and fell into canals or emergency water containers. It was easy to get lost if you went out at night, so finding your way home became difficult.

Because of all these problems, kerbs and steps were painted white. White circles were painted around telephone and pillar boxes and any trees that might be where people would bump into them. This helped a bit, but now there is very dim street lighting and people are allowed to carry a torch that must be dimmed with tissue paper and shone downwards. The No 8 batteries you need for these small torches are always in short supply.

Father and I play a game of Snakes and Ladders. We are so involved in the board game that neither of us notices Tilly pulling Mother's knitting off the sofa. By the time that we do, she has got the ball of wool, unwound some of it, and is pulling it across the floor with the knitting and needles dragging behind. I rescue the knitting, much to Tillys disapproval and go and get my wind up tin car, which I've had since I was about five years old. Tilly loves to chase the little car around the room and never tires of this game.

The car whizzes all over the place, only stopping when it runs into a piece of furniture. Then, Tilly pounces on it, but she doesn't like the taste of the cold metal. It's the movement of the car that attracts her.

Father returns from the kitchen with two cups of cocoa on a tray. I've just set the car off across the floor, and as he tries to come through the door, Tilly shoots right in front of him after the car. Taken by surprise, he just manages to hang on to the tray and stop the cocoa from spilling everywhere.

"William! For goodness sake put the car away. That cat is mad enough without you making her worse!" he says.

Time for bed. No sirens have gone off so far. I hope that no planes come tonight because I worry about Mother out there trying to do her job. I say goodnight to Father. He will wait up like he usually does, until Mother gets home, which should be in about another couple of hours, although, she is often late because it's not the sort of job where you can just stop at a certain time if you are needed urgently.

5

No lovely eggs for breakfast this morning. It's back to National Loaf. Mother looks tired after her Air Raid Patrol duty.

She cleans my cut knee and says "It will be alright without a bandage now. Let the air get to your skin and it will soon heal"

"I hope that you don't mind me asking, but why hasn't Father been called up?"

There, I've said it.

"No, I don't mind William. I thought that you might ask me that question one day. Father can't join the National Service because of his health. He tried to join up as soon as the war started, but he failed the medical examination. Your Father has poor vision and his lungs are damaged. This was caused when he served as a soldier in the First World War.

She notices my look of surprise.

"You didn't know Father was is the First World War did you? He never talks about it, so you probably thought that he would have been too young to be called up. Well, he was too young, but because his older brothers had gone off to fight, he wanted to do the same, and towards the end of the war in 1918, he managed to get in by pretending that he was older than he actually was. At fifteen years of age, he was sent over to France to fight in the trenches and he hadn't been there for very long, when he was injured in a gas attack. He has permanent damage as a result of those injuries. You may have noticed how strict he is about reminding us to always take our gas masks with us everywhere we go. That's because he knows what it is like to be hurt by gas"

Poor Father. I knew that there must be a good reason why he wasn't in the National Service. I know that he wears glasses and has a cough that never seems to go away. I also remember that he gets out of breath very quickly when we play football in the park. I suppose that's because of his injuries.

I say how sorry I am to hear about what happened to Father.

Then Mother says

"I will tell Father that I have spoken to you about his injuries, but it's probably best not to speak of this subject to him unless he mentions it. It hasn't been easy for him, having his health ruined at such a young age, and now with another war, it brings back memories of what he went through with the last one. His work in the Fire Service has made him feel that he is helping with the war, although, by rights, he shouldn't really be in that with his weak lungs.

I feel proud of both my parents, doing the best that they can in this time of trouble.

6

Joe's latest nickname for me is "Teachers Pet" because Miss Adams said that I showed initiative repairing the damage to my books which he messed up.

I've had enough of him so I tell him to shut up and also that my Father is not a "Conchie"

"Says who?" he asks.

"Me. He was a soldier in the First World War and he was badly injured so he's not fit enough to be in this one"

"I don't believe you. You're making it up. He looks alright to me"

"No I'm not, it's the truth. He got gassed and now his eyes and lungs are damaged."

"Well, you're still a sissy" We're in the playground and he shoves me against a wall.

Whack!

That's me punching him. It's the first time that I've hit another boy and I don't like doing it, but he's gone too far. I suppose that's how wars start. Someone behaves badly and you have to stop them, even if you don't like the way in which you have to do it.

Joe seems quite shocked that I hit him. I wait for him to hit me back, but he doesn't, so I walk away half expecting him to run up behind me and knock me over, but he doesn't. Maybe because I stood up to him, he will now leave me alone.

Coming home through the front gate after school, I look out

for Tilly. She's usually waiting for me, but today, I can't see her anywhere. Perhaps she is in the kitchen with Mother.

"Hello William. Have you had a good day?"

Mother is darning socks, trying to make them last a bit longer.

"Yes, I had a good day" I reply. I'm not going to tell her about hitting Joe. Mother definitely wouldn't approve. "Have you seen Tilly?"

"Not since this morning. She was in the garden, down by the air raid shelter. She's probably out hunting for mice"

I go into the garden to look for Tilly. I look everywhere, but there's no sign of her. That's very odd. I always feed her as soon as I come home from school and I'm sure that she knows the time of day because she never misses a feed.

I search the house from top to bottom and check inside cupboards in case she has got shut in. Once, when we first had her, she crawled into Mother's wardrobe and fell asleep there.

Tilly isn't anywhere and I'm starting to get worried.

Father comes home from work and we have our meal. Still no Tilly. She's always here with us at this time, never missing a chance to try to scrounge a bit of food.

I finish my dinner as quickly as possible, so that I can get back to my search.

"I'm just going along the road to look for Tilly" I tell Mother and Father.

"Don't go too far. It will be getting dark soon" says Mother.

I walk all the way to the end of our road and back, then pass our house and go in the other direction. There are a few cats to be seen but none of them is Tilly. Where can she be?

Tonight Father is on duty with the Fire Service. Mother and I put up the blackout curtains as we do every night. The horrid black curtains make the house seem miserable and gloomy. Blackout time is announced on the radio and in the newspapers – it varies according to the time of year. It's confusing in the mornings. Sometimes, I wake up and because no light shows through the window, I think that it is earlier than it actually is. For my last birthday, I got a little alarm clock, so now I've taken to setting the alarm to wake me up.

I'm really worried about Tilly. It's too late to look for her anymore tonight. She has never stayed away all night since she's been with us.

Mother suggests that we play a game of cards, so we play Snap. I know that she is trying to keep my mind off Tilly, but it doesn't work.

After our cup of bedtime cocoa, I take a quick look outside the back door to see if Tilly is out there. She isn't and there's nothing more that I can do tonight but go to bed.

"William, the sirens are sounding" Mother is standing by my bed.

Oh no, not tonight. Aloud I say "Alright, I'll get ready"

Instead of my dressing gown, I grab my thick overcoat and some warm socks. It's so cold in the shelter now that winter is coming.

Mother and I run down the garden over the frozen ground.

In the shelter, we hear planes passing overhead, but no sounds of bombs falling. I say that I wonder where Tilly is. Mother says not to worry, cats often wander off for a few days and then come back. She tells me that she had a cat when she was a girl and that was always disappearing only to return again. I hope that she is right and that Tilly will come back to us.

7

The night passes slowly and I don't get much sleep.

Father comes off duty and says that no bombs fell near us during the night. This cheers me a bit. I'm determined to keep looking for Tilly. There will be time when school finishes.

At school, Joe ignores me and keeps out of my way. He will probably find someone else to pick on now. I pity the poor soul, whoever it is.

I don't usually mind lessons. In fact, I think most of them are interesting, but my mind is not on learning today. I just want to get out of school and find Tilly. She must be somewhere.

When school finally ends, I rush all the way home. Tilly hasn't returned and Mother has left a note saying that she is at the shops, so I leave the house and walk up and down the road. When I reach the bombed houses, I wonder if Tilly could have wandered into one of them. There are still bits of rooms visible although the roofs have gone.

My parents have always told me never to go into bombed houses because the buildings are dangerous and likely to collapse. I know that I should heed their advice, but I don't.

No one is about, so I make my way round to the back of the first house and start to climb over a pile of rubble, which is all that is left of the kitchen. I find a door that leads to the hall. In the hall, a staircase is still in one piece, leading to the floor above.

"Tilly, Tilly" I call out. She often meows when I call her name, but there is no answer.

It's quite creepy in the house, but I've got this far, so I might as well take a quick look around before I go.

I start to climb the stairs. They creak and groan and wobble a bit. I've got halfway up, when, suddenly, there is a loud bang from one of the upstairs rooms. Now, I'm getting rather frightened. Perhaps this wasn't such a good idea after all. Maybe the house is starting to fall down or maybe there is someone else upstairs. The noise was too loud to have been made by such a small cat as Tilly.

I decide to go back down the stairs before the whole house gives way. Then, I hear another noise- this time it's a faint cry. There is someone upstairs. Should I go and look to see whom it is, or should I go and get help?

A big lump of plaster drops from the ceiling onto the hall floor and a cloud of dust rises up. I close my eyes for a few moments to stop the dust getting in them. I know that it's really dangerous to be here. I must move very gently so as not to make things worse.

When I'm almost at the bottom of the staircase, I hear the cry again.

"Who's there?" I call. No reply.

I have to go back. I'm sure that someone needs help.

Treading as softly as possible, I manage to reach the landing.

"Who's there?" I call again. Nothing. Why don't they answer?

To my right is a door. The door is hanging off its top hinges, half- falling across the landing. I crawl under the door and find myself in what used to be a bedroom. Only three walls remain. The ceiling and far wall have gone, just sky above my head. There is some broken furniture - a wardrobe lying on its side and a bed covered in bits of plaster and bricks. The floor doesn't look very safe. There are gaping holes where floorboards have collapsed.

Then, there is a noise, which I think is coming from behind the fallen wardrobe. A sort of creaking sound.

Not trusting the floorboards, I keep my back against the wall and slide along towards the corner where the wardrobe is. It's a big double wardrobe like the sort my parents have.

When I reach the wardrobe, I peer over it to see what is behind it, and get quite a shock when I find a boy there. He seems equally shocked to see me and we both gasp with surprise.

"I'm stuck" are the first words he says to me.

I can see only the upper part of his body and then I realise that he must be stuck because his legs have gone through the floorboards.

"Are you in pain? I'll try to help you" I say.

"No, I don't feel too bad. A bit sore and scratched. The floor broke and I fell through up to my waist. I can't get out"

I climb over the wardrobe and stand in the small space next to the boy. I notice that he looks about the same age as myself.

"I'll try to pull you back through the hole" I say, and putting my hands under his arms, I pull as hard as I can, but it's no good, I'm not strong enough.

"I can't do it. Don't worry, I'll go and get some help"

"No, you mustn't" the boy almost yells at me.

"Why? I won't be long and you'll soon be out of here" I say.

"You don't understand. I've been looting the house and they hang people for looting" he says.

It's then that I see a bag on the floor beside the boy. I'd heard about looters going into bombed houses to look for anything to steal, but I hadn't expected that this boy was one of them.

"What are you doing that for?" is all that I can think of to say.

"It's a long story. I know it's wrong and I don't like having to steal, but I've got to get something worth selling so that I can buy some food with the money. I'm starving and it's said that you can get most things on the Black Market if you have money"

I'd heard about the Black Market. People steal clothing and food from warehouses or articles from bombed houses and offer them for sale, usually at high prices because they know how much these things are in short supply.

"Don't your parents look after you?" I ask.

"My Mother left my Father when I was a baby, so he and my Gran brought me up, but now my Father's in a Prisoner of War camp in Germany and my Gran has died, so I've been put into an orphanage. I didn't much like it there, so I ran away. I've been sleeping in empty houses and stealing any food that I can lay my hands on, but it's not easy trying to survive with this war going on"

I'm shocked by the boy's story. He seems to be having a really hard time.

"I'll get my Father. He will be able to pull you free, and if I put back the things that you've taken, no one will know that you were looting" I say.

"Would you? I'd be most grateful. I did feel a bit rotten taking other peoples things, but I couldn't think of any other way to manage on my own and I'm so hungry. By the way, my name's Tom Finch, what's yours?"

"William Turner"

"Pleased to meet you William" he holds out his hand to shake mine, then looks at the grime on it.

"Sorry, I'm not usually this grubby. Haven't had much of a chance to wash properly"

"Never mind. I'm pleased to meet you Tom and we'll soon have you out of here" I shake his hand.

Tom gives me the bag and tells me where he took the contents from.

"There's only a few pieces of jewellery that I found in a box in the wardrobe. I hadn't been in the house for very long when I heard you downstairs. I tried to hide behind the wardrobe, but the floor gave way and I ended up like this"

I put the jewellery back and say that I'll go and get my Father.

"Mind how you go. This place is very unsafe" says Tom.

Although I want to get home as quickly as possible, I have to make myself tread carefully. If I fall through the floor, Tom and I will both be stuck here and we might not be found for ages if at all.

I get safely down to the ground floor and call up to Tom.

"I'll bring help soon"

Now that I'm out of the house, I run as fast as I can down the road. The light is fading as evening comes, so I want to get Father's help as soon as possible because I know that it will be even more dangerous trying to free Tom in the dark.

I burst into the kitchen to find Mother laying the table for dinner.

"William. I was just starting to get worried about you. You know that we don't like you staying out when it's getting dark" she says.

"I'm sorry Mother, but this is really important. I need Fathers help. There's a boy trapped in one of the bombed houses. He's fallen through the floorboards and we must save him now"

"Good gracious! Is he badly hurt?"

"I don't think that he is hurt much, but the house is unsafe and it could collapse if we don't get him out soon"

Mother hurries into the sitting room. I hear her talking quickly to Father.

Father comes into the kitchen, puts on his coat and takes his torch from the shelf.

"Lets go William. I will be speaking to you later about how you came to be in that house. You know very well that we have forbidden you to enter such places because of things like this happening"

"Yes Father" I reply. I know that I'm going to be in for a ticking off, but for the moment Father is more concerned with saving Tom.

Mother says that she will come to help but Father tells her to stay here.

"We don't want too many people in that building" he says.

"Please take care Harold" Mother looks very worried.

"Don't worry" Father gives Mother a kiss on the cheek.

"Come on William"

Father and I hurry down the road. It's almost dark now with just a bit of daylight left in the sky.

At the bombed house, I lead Father round to the back and we climb over the kitchen rubble to reach the hall door.

In the hall, I call out to Tom.

"Tom, I'm back. My Father is here to get you out"

Tom answers.

"Hello. It's good to hear your voice. There have been a few funny noises. I think the house is falling down" he sounds very scared.

"I'm coming up to get you. It won't be long now" Father calls.

He asks me to explain exactly where Tom is, so I do this and also remind him that the floor in the bedroom looks very unsafe. I'm worried because Father is much heavier than I am and the floor might not be able to take his weight.

"Stay here and do not follow me" he says.

Then, he starts to make his way up the rickety staircase with the help of his torch, as, now, it is quite dark in the hall. He goes slowly and carefully, testing each stair with his foot before putting all his weight on it.

I have my little torch on, so I can see him until he reaches the landing. Then, he is lost to me and all that I can do is to wait and listen for any sounds.

It's gone very quiet. Father must be in the bedroom by now, providing that he can squeeze under the door. I found it not too difficult, but he is bigger than I am.

Suddenly, from above comes a loud bang.

I call out

"Are you alright?"

"Yes William. I had to move the wardrobe so that I can pull Tom back up through the floorboards." Father replies. It's reassuring to know that he is with Tom now.

More creaks and bangs, then what seems like hours, but can only have been a few minutes pass, and there is a beam of light at the top of the stairs. Father and Tom have made it out of the bedroom without harm and have only got to get down the staircase now.

I shine my torch upwards and see Tom coming slowly down towards me. He holds the banister rail and although he is probably trying to go as gently as possible, he looks very stiff in his movements. I expect that he must be very sore from falling through the floorboards.

The light from my torch helps Tom find his way down. Father stays at the top of the stairs. He probably doesn't trust the staircase to support the weight of both him and Tom on it at the same time.

Tom reaches the hall and gives a sigh of relief.

"Your Father's great. He pulled me out easily. Thank you so much for saving me"

Father comes down the stairs, and luckily, the staircase holds strong enough for him.

"Right, let's get out of here" he says, shining the torch in front of us.

Back we go over the rubble, round to the front of the house and then onto the pavement. I help Tom, who seems to be flagging a bit.

"My legs went a bit numb hanging through the floor, but they are getting better now" he says.

Father asks where Tom lives. Tom gives me a frightened look. I have to think quickly what to say because I don't want to get him into trouble.

"Could we please take Tom to our house. It's near and he must be tired and sore. I'm sure that Mother will make him more comfortable."

"Alright, but his parents will have to be contacted as soon as we have cleaned him up and dressed his cuts" Father has just noticed how scruffy Tom's appearance is.

"Oh, I'm fine really. I can make my own way home now" Tom starts to turn away, but I grab his arm.

"It's ok Tom, you can come with us. Mother will be pleased to help you and she'll give you something to eat if you're hungry" I say.

Tom looks torn between making an excuse to get away and the

thought of a longed for meal. It seems that the meal wins because he says

"Are you sure?"

"Of course. We live only just down the road"

Father walks on ahead of us. I walk beside Tom who is still moving very stiffly, and whisper to him

"I won't give you away"

"I didn't think that you would, but I don't want to go back to that orphanage" he whispers.

"We'll think of a way to stop you having to go back there, but first, you must let my Mother dress your cuts and give you some food, and you look as if you could do with a good rest."

Tom is too exhausted to object. I'm sure that he is much more shaken up than he pretends. It's been quite an ordeal for him.

Mother seems relieved to see us all home in one piece. She takes one look at Tom and immediately starts fussing over him.

"You poor boy. What a state you're in. Come and sit down and have a cup of cocoa. That will warm you up"

Tom slumps down on a kitchen chair and gratefully accepts the cocoa, which Mother produces in no time at all. Cocoa is Mother's answer to all upsets. I'm sure that she put the milk to boil on the gas cooker as soon as Father and I set off to rescue Tom, just so that it would be ready in time for our return.

Tom drinks the cocoa as if he hasn't had anything to drink for ages, which I suppose is probably true.

"Thank you. That was lovely" he says, licking his lips to savour every bit of the cocoa.

"Now, if you come with me, I'll show you where the bathroom is and you can wash your cuts before I put some ointment on them"

Tom follows Mother out of the kitchen and while they are gone, I take the chance to talk to Father about Tom's situation. I'm sure that my parents will know what to do to help him.

I quickly rush through how I came to find Tom in the bombed house, but I don't mention the looting. Do they really hang people who loot houses? I don't know. Anyway, Toms not a thief, he was only trying to survive. I tell Father all about Tom's Gran dying and his Father being in a prisoner of war camp.

"We've got to help him Father"

"Alright William, calm down. Of course we will see what can be done to help Tom, but I will have to notify the orphanage in the morning as to his whereabouts. He can stay here tonight"

Mother and Tom come back into the kitchen. Tom has washed his face and hands and now looks a bit cleaner. Mother opens the first aid box, gets out the ointment and bandages, then tells Tom to lift up his shirt. There are ugly marks around his waist where the broken floorboards scratched him and also some nasty bruises starting to form. She gently dresses the cuts, then says

"William, go and find some of your clothes for Tom to wear. He has torn his shirt and trousers and as you are both about the same size, your clothes should fit him"

Tom and I go to my bedroom to get the clothes. While he is putting on the clothes, I tell him that I have spoken to my Father about his situation and that Father will try to help him. Tom is really pleased when I say that he can stay with us tonight.

"I suppose that I couldn't have gone on living rough, so I'll just have to put up with going back to the orphanage until the war ends and my Father comes home" he says.

I hope that we do win the war and that Tom's Father does get home again. The longer the war goes on, the more I wonder how it will all end.

Mother calls up to us that dinner is ready.

It's warm and cosy in the kitchen. The food smells good. Woolton pie again, plus a sausage each and the ever present National loaf.

"I'm sure that we can stretch the food to four instead of three portions" she says.

Tom looks at the food as if it's a banquet. He hastily takes a seat at the table saying

"It's really kind of you to let me stay here tonight and give me some food"

We are all hungry, but Tom must be the hungriest. He eats so quickly and even manages three slices of the loaf. I notice Mother wink at Father as they watch him eat. Father smiles back at her. It's a happy time, and, for a while, I have forgotten the reason why I went into the bombed house – Tilly. Although I'm glad that I found Tom and was able to help him, I still miss Tilly, and now, I'm beginning to think that I will never see her again.

I help to clear the plates when we have eaten, then Mother opens one of the jars of plums which she preserved in the summer when Mrs Thomas let her pick some of the fruit from her plum tree. This is a real treat. The plums are gorgeous, all juicy and sweet. It's difficult to eat them without the juice running down your chin.

"That was absolutely lovely. Thank you Mrs Turner" says Tom after we have eaten a whole jar of plums between the four of us.

We finish with cups of tea and Tom and I do the washing up, whilst Mother goes to make up a bed for Tom in my room. We have a little folding bed that is kept in a cupboard so this will be ideal for Tom.

The blackout curtains are up. No air raid sirens have gone off yet. Maybe we will get a peaceful night but you can never be sure.

We are all tired, so instead of playing games or listening to the radio, Mother suggests that Tom and I should try to get some sleep.

"I'll check outside to see if Tilly's back before your father and I go up to bed" she says, knowing that I did so last night.

Mother has laid a pair of my pyjamas on Tom's bed for him and also put hot water bottles in our beds.

"I never thought that I would be sleeping in a warm bed tonight. It feels so nice" says Tom, snuggling down beneath the blankets.

I notice that on top of the pile of clothes he has taken off, is a small photograph and I ask who is the person in the photograph.

"It's my Father" Tom proudly hands the photograph over for me to look at.

I see a man with a moustache and a pleasant face, wearing an army uniform.

"Father was with some other soldiers on a mission. They were dropped by parachute, but the Germans were waiting for them and the men were either captured or killed. Luckily, Father wasn't injured but he has been a prisoner of war for quite a while. I write to him and get letters back. It seems that he is being treated fairly well."

I hope that Tom's Father is being treated well. I remember over-hearing Mrs Thomas talking to Mother about her son Frank, who is in the British army over in France. She said that he always writes cheery letters to her, saying things aren't too bad, but she is sure that it's much worse than he leads her to believe. "He's only trying not to worry me, and I suppose that I do the same with him, telling him that we haven't been bothered with many bombs, when in truth, there have been quite a few near misses here lately. We're just trying to keep each others spirits up" she said. Perhaps Tom's Father is trying to keep Tom's spirits up.

I lean over from my bed to hand the photograph back to Tom. He gently places it on the pile of clothes, then snuggles down into the bed again. The photograph must be his most prized possession. I can imagine how awful I would feel if my Father was a prisoner of war and all I had to remember him by was a photograph. In a way, I'm glad that Father can't join the war. He could have ended up like Tom's Father. Poor Tom, and poor Mr Finch.

I turn out the little light beside my bed.

"Goodnight Tom" I say, but there is no answer, just his steady breathing. Tom is already asleep. It's been quite a day.

8 I'm in the bombed house and it's falling down around me. It's very frightening because I can't get out. Every time I find a door and open it, bits of the house come crashing down to block the way. I'm choking with the dust and the noise of the house collapsing sounds like people scream-ing for help.

I wake up, sweating and shaking, confused for a few moments Then, I realise that it was only a dream. I'm still in my bedroom and Tom is in the bed opposite me, making little snoring noises. All is normal, well as normal as anything can be in a time like this.

Putting my torch on and shining it at the alarm clock, I see that it's early, 4.30am. No school today, its Saturday and breakfast won't be till 8.30, so I might as well go back to sleep. I hope that I don't get another bad dream.

"William, William" I must have dropped off to sleep again, because now I'm aware of Mother standing beside the bed calling my name.

"Is it an air raid?" I ask, trying to wake myself, ready to rush to the shelter.

"No, nothing's wrong. I just want you to come downstairs with me now" she says.

I put on my dressing gown and slippers and follow her down-stairs to the kitchen.

The table is laid for breakfast and the kettle is starting to boil on the gas cooker. Nothing seems out of place.

Then Mother points to a blanket lying on the floor in front of the coal stove. I can't believe my eyes. On the blanket, spread out on her side is Tilly! And not just Tilly! Beside her is a tiny tabby kitten. The kitten is sleeping, snuggled up to Tilly who has a contented look on her face. I bend down and stroke her under her chin, which she loves, and I can hear her purring. It seems a miracle that she is back with us, and to have a little kitten as well, is almost too much to wish for. Mother bends down next to me and says

"I came downstairs to make a cup of tea at 7 o' clock and heard a cat crying outside the back door. When I took a look, I found Tilly holding this little kitten in her mouth. It's obvious that she is its mother"

So this was the reason why Tilly has been extra hungry and looking fatter – she was expecting kittens.

"Don't cats usually have more than one kitten?" I ask Mother

"Usually, but it's possible that Tilly had others that didn't survive. I've looked all over the garden and I can't see any more babies" says Mother.

Well, it's lucky that she has this little one.

I just want to sit here by the warmth of the stove, staring at Tilly and the kitten. Then Tom comes into the room, still yawning from his long sleep, so I show him what all the excitement is about.

The kitten wakes and makes a meowing noise, then starts suckling from Tilly. I wonder where Tilly went to have her baby. Perhaps she wanted some place private, but now she has brought the kitten to show us, so she must feel that this is her home. I hope that she won't go away again.

"We will be able to keep little Titch, won't we?" I ask Mother, realising as I say this, that I've already given the kitten a name. Titch – I don't know if it's a boy or a girl, but I think that the name would do for either.

"Maybe. We will have to speak to your father. You know that he's not too fond of cats" says Mother. She is making as much fuss of the kitten as Tom and I am, so I'm pretty sure that she wouldn't mind another cat in the house.

"Where is Father?" I ask. He's not at work today because it's Saturday.

"He went to the orphanage" she replies.

I glance at Tom and see the smile on his face as he is stroking the kitten suddenly disappear to be replaced by a frown.

"I thought that this would be too good to last" he mutters.

"Does Tom have to go back there? Can't he stay with us?" I can't bear to think of Tom being sent back to the orphanage.

"It will have to be up to the orphanage to decide. They are responsible for Tom. Your Father and I are quite prepared to offer Tom a home with us, and he has gone to tell the people at the orphanage, so we will have to wait until he returns to find out if they have agreed. Now, why don't you boys go and get dressed and I'll cook us some scrambled eggs on toast. I've still got some dried eggs left from the rations"

Dear Mother. She is doing her best to keep Tom's mind off the fact that he might have to leave us.

We go up to my bedroom. Tom sits on his bed, picks up the photograph of his Father and says

"You know William, before this war started, I had a happy home life with my Gran and my Father. Gran was a bit like your Mother. She looked after me so well and she was such a kind person. Now everything has changed"

"Cheer up Tom. Perhaps you will be able to stay with us" I have to try to keep his spirits up. I hate to see him as downhearted as this, but I don't really think that anything I can say will help much. "Let's get ready for breakfast. Scrambled eggs sound good, even if they are only dried ones"

Mother has done us proud. Scrambled eggs on toast and extra toast spread with blackberry jam, which she made from the blackberries we found growing at the edge of the recreation ground. No one used to bother much to pick the berries before the war started, but now they go quite quickly. Home made jam tastes a whole lot better than the shop bought stuff.

Although Tom's appetite is as good as ever, he is much less jolly than he was when we all sat round the table last night. He appears to be listening for any noise that shows Father has returned - waiting to find out what will happen to him. It's horrible.

There's a knock on the front door, but it's only Mrs Thomas asking to borrow Mother's vacuum cleaner because her one has broken.

Mother introduces Mrs Thomas to Tom and tells her how I came to find him. Then it's time to admire Tilly and Titch. Tilly is washing her baby, licking it all over whilst Titch wriggles around on the blanket.

At this moment, Father comes through the back door. We all stop talking at once and look towards him.

"It's alright Tom. You can stay here with us if you want to" he says, and these words light up Tom's face into a big grin.

"Of course I want to. I promise that I'll be no trouble and I'll help around the house" he says.

"Well, that's settled then" says Mother. "We must get some things together for Tom if he is to stay with us. He will need a few more clothes and I'll have to register with the shopkeeper for his food rations."

Tom and I do the washing up while Mother goes to the shops. She will probably be gone all morning, because you always have to queue for hours for everything you need.

After we've finished in the kitchen, Father says that Tom should write to his Father telling him where he will be staying. "I shall put a letter in with yours, introducing myself to your Father" he says.

I'm really excited that Tom can stay with us. Life doesn't seem so bad now that I've got a new friend. All I need to make it even better is to persuade Father to let me keep Titch.

No time like the present, so here goes.

"Father. Please may I keep Titch?"

"Titch, who's Titch?" he asks.

"Er, it's the name I've given Tilly's kitten"

Father looks at me very seriously, then says

"William. We still haven't spoken about you defying my orders about not going into bombed houses. Why on earth should I let you keep yet another cat after you disobeyed me and put yourself at great risk of injury wandering off hunting for a cat?"

"Yes Father. I'm really sorry that I disobeyed you"

It's not going very well. I fear that I might be told to get rid of Tilly, as well as the kitten.

"It is fortunate that something good has come out of all this with Tom being found, but that might not have been the case. If that cat runs off again, you are not, and I repeat not to go looking for her in such places, do you understand me?"

"Yes Father. I will do as you say" From what he has just said, it seems that Tilly is not going to be sent away, so I push my luck a bit further.

"But, please can we keep Titch?"

He still looks very serious, but then he gives a sigh and says

"I suppose that if you have already given the kitten a name, then, yes you may keep it. Now, off you go Tom and write that letter to your Father"

I think, if the truth be told, that Father is becoming as fond of the cats as Mother and I am.

9 My bedroom is getting rather full. Tom has a corner of it for himself. There is a little bookcase, which Mrs Thomas has lent him, full of books that belonged to her son Frank when he was a boy. We are enjoying reading the books. On top of the bookcase is the photograph of Tom's Father, safely in a frame that Mother found for it. Tom says everyone has been so kind and it's almost like being in his own home again.

Tilly and Titch (who is a girl) have a basket beside my bed. Titch grows bigger by the day and will soon be able to climb onto my bed. She swings on the bedspread and hides underneath it, pouncing out onto the unsuspecting Tilly, who doesn't like this very much and swipes Titch with her paw, then hisses at her. Soon Titch will need a basket of her own, for I think that Tilly is going to say in cat language "Get out!" and claim her basket back.

If my bedroom is crowded, then the Air Raid Shelter is even more so. Father built a bunk for Tom and he hasn't complained about the two cats being taken in there with us every time there is a raid.

There have been quite a few doodlebug raids lately. At one end of our road, is a roundabout with a big oak tree growing in the middle. Three other oak trees grow along Forest Way, which is one of the roads that lead from the roundabout. These trees are known locally as Matthew, Mark, Luke and John, named from the Bible, and are said to be about six hundred years old. I've climbed the one in the middle of the roundabout. It's easy to climb because the trunk divides low down and you have to scramble up only a little way to reach a place where you can sit amongst the branches. Most of the children round here play on the trees. Sometimes, we throw ropes over the lowest branches and make swings.

One evening, last week, the air raid sirens went off and we ran into the shelter. We could hear the sound of a doodlebug overhead, then all went quiet as the engine stopped, so we knew that the bomb was going to fall. It was very frightening. When the explosion came, everything in the shelter shook, including all of us, and I knew that the bomb had landed nearby. More doodlebugs came over as we huddled in the shelter and the night seemed to go on forever. It was awful. I felt sure that we would all die.

Well, we survived the night, but others didn't. A house in Forest Way received a direct hit from one of the bombs. It soon got round the neighbourhood next morning that all of the family who lived there had been killed.

Tom didn't go to school the day after the air raid. He had a bad cold, so Mother said it would be best for him to stay at home. Being in the damp Anderson shelter hadn't helped his cough, so I left him to get some sleep whilst I went off to school.

I wish that I had not walked down Forest Way to go to school. I could quite easily have gone the other way through the recreation ground and missed what I ended up seeing. It was the most terrible sight that I've ever seen. The house had just vanished. All that was left was a gaping hole where it should have been with piles of rubble and blackened timber which was still smoking and giving off a horrible smell that made me feel sick.

Then, I noticed that one of the four oak trees, which had been outside the house, was also burnt. The fire must have spread and caught it alight. The proud old tree that had stood for many centuries, would now have to be chopped down, and I knew that for me, the place where I had spent so many happy hours in games of play, could never be the same again. Now, it was a sad place, touched by death and destruction.

And there was something else that will always stay in my mind – the doll's pram. Amongst all the broken remains of the house, lying on its side, was this doll's pram, and beside the pram, wrapped in a blanket, was a baby doll. I hadn't known the family who lived in the house. They had moved in only a short time ago, but I remember seeing a little girl pushing the pram past our house. I remember because she had spoken to me.

"Do you want to see my baby?" she asked.

I said yes and the little girl lifted the doll out of the pram and showed it to me.

"Her name's Daisy"

I remember saying something like "That's a nice name". I wasn't really interested in the doll, but I could tell that it meant a lot to the little girl. She was only about six years old, slightly built with fair hair tied in bunches and she had freckles on her nose.

Tucking the doll back into the pram, she said

"Daisy's my first baby. I want lots of babies. I think babies are lovely don't you?" and off she went down the road talking to the doll.

I stood staring at the pram and "Daisy" and I felt tears running down my face. I was thinking that the little girl was still not much more than a baby herself – now she would never grow up, would never have a real baby of her own.

I scrambled over the rubble, picked up the doll and dragged the pram back onto the pavement. Then, using some spit and a handkerchief, I cleaned Daisy's face, which was covered in soot, and laid her in the pram. One of the men who were clearing up the mess came towards me.

"Best move along now lad. There's nothing you can do here. I'll take care of the doll" he said, patting me gently on the back. "Her name's Daisy" I told him.

I walked on to school, still crying. I didn't seem to be able to stop. All I could think of was that poor girl and her family, their lives so cruelly ended in a night of bombing

Priscilla Winn.

I didn't even know her name, but, later, I was to find out what it was. At school, in assembly, our headmaster, Mr Gregson, made us all say a prayer for Alice Stevens and her family who had died in the house. I hadn't noticed that Alice went to our school. She must have been in the infants and the infants have a different playground to the one used by us older children.

"Fat lot of good praying will do" said Joe, when assembly was over, and, for once, I found myself agreeing with him. Praying wouldn't bring Alice Stevens back to life.

10 It's December and Christmas day will be in two weeks time. In June, when so many of our soldiers invaded Normandy, most people were saying that the war would be over by Christmas, but it's not. We are all trying to make the best of things. Mother has started putting up decorations and Father went to the woods to cut some holly. The sitting room looks cheery with all the decorations. Tom and I got quite thirsty licking the sticky paper to make the paper chains. We found the paper for the chains in the loft. It had been up there for years, forgotten and left over from a Christmas gone by. The stickiness has worn off a bit, and because of this, every now and then, a chain breaks and falls down. It was funny – the other evening, Father had nodded off to sleep and a chain broke and fell on him. He didn't wake up, just twitched his nose in his sleep. Another time, one landed where Tilly was sitting. She thought it was a great game and began pulling the chain all over the place, until we had to stop her before she could destroy it.

Mother keeps a small piece of holly to decorate the Christmas pudding. She likes to do everything as nice as possible for Christmas. One of the tips that she got from the Ministry of Food leaflets is how to decorate holly by dipping it in a strong solution of Epsom Salts. When the salts dry, the holly is beautifully frosted and looks good lying on the plate with the pudding. She has a recipe for Christmas pudding made without eggs and another for mock cream made with margarine, sugar, dried milk powder and a little milk.

It's no good expecting turkey for Christmas dinner as families had before the war. You just can't get turkey, so instead we have "Murkey" which is stuffed mutton. We have had murkey every Christmas since 1941. It's not bad, certainly better than the corned beef hash or spam fritters that are our usual meat meals. There are still fresh vegetables from the garden and Mother will make a rhubarb crumble from the rhubarb that was grown in the air raid shelter. This year, the Ministry of Food has issued

"Christmas Treats" Each family gets an extra half a pound of sugar, half a pound of margarine, eight pennyworth of meat and half a pound of sweets added to the rations.

The blackout is over because the Germans now use their pilotless planes for all the bombing. For the first time in four years, churches have been allowed to light up their stained glass windows. There's a church at the end of our road. The other day, I stood gazing up at the coloured window which shows Jesus on the cross, and I thought, if there is a God, then why does he let such horrible things happen? Why did he let little Alice Stevens die? Why can't he do something to end this war?

I saved some of my pocket money each week for two months to buy presents for everyone. Everything in the shops is so expensive. Mother has a tiny bottle of scent, Father two handkerchiefs with his initial on them, Tom a tin whistle, Titch a knitted blanket that took ages to make, and last but by no means least, Tilly has a little bell which I've tied onto a piece of ribbon. The bell makes a tinkling noise that Mother and Father will probably be sick and tired of before Christmas is over. I don't know what presents I will get. What I'd really like is a train set, but I don't think there is much hope of getting one. Train sets are very expensive and in short supply. As long as I don't get a jigsaw puzzle, I'll be happy. I have never liked the things and can't see the point of spending hours trying to make up a picture that you can already see on the box cover.

11 Christmas morning. It's good to have Tom here with us, but I'm sure that he would rather be spending the day with his Father if it were possible. He posted a card to his Father about three weeks ago because we don't know how long it takes to reach the prisoner of war camp. Tom hasn't heard back from his Father yet, which I know he was hoping to do so. Every time there has been some post through our door, he's been the first to collect it from the doormat. It's horrible to see how sad he looks when there's no letter for him.

Mother told Tom that the Red Cross takes parcels of food to prisoners of war so that they can have a treat at Christmas and this seems to have cheered him up a bit.

Even though Tom and I are really too old for Christmas stockings, Mother insisted that we hang up the two she made on the end of our beds. Although I say we are too old, I still enjoy sorting out the assortment of things that she gets to fill the stockings. There are home made sweets from the extra sugar ration, little whistles that you blow into to make the paper tube unwind with a noise, knitted socks, handkerchiefs, a comic, notepad and a pencil with a rubber at the other end, a ruler, and a tiny paint tin with four colours of paint inside.

Tom and I lay all the gifts from the stockings on our beds. Then I give him my present.

"Merry Christmas Tom" I say.

He seems really pleased with the tin whistle and starts trying to play a tune.

"I'll need to practise a bit won't I?" he laughs as I cover my ears with my hands.

Tom has a present for me. When I unwrap the present, I find a copy of "Treasure Island"

"Your Mother told me that it's your favourite book and that you gave up the one you had to the Salvage Drive" he says

Opening the book, I see that Tom has written inside "For my best friend William Turner from Tom Finch, Christmas 1944"

I thank Tom and say what a lovely present it is.

"It's not new of course. I haven't any money to buy books. I saw it in Mrs Thomas's bookcase and I said that you had given up your book. She said take it, but I couldn't just do that, so I suggested that if I did some odd jobs for her, that would make me feel like I had sort of paid for the book" he says.

What a good idea. That word initiative comes into my mind.

The weathers been very nasty since 19th December, freezing fog every day. I draw back the curtains to look outside, and find that it's the same today. I'd hoped for snow like you used to see on Christmas cards, but it hardly ever snows on Christmas Day. Not many cards get sent at Christmas time now because of the paper shortage, but I always try to make one for my parents with a sheet of paper from my notebook.

Tom and I get dressed and go downstairs to the kitchen where Mother is getting everything ready for Christmas dinner. I had planned to help her peel the vegetables, but she has already done them. Never mind, Tom and I will do the washing up for her after dinner so that she can have a rest.

Father has lit the fire in the sitting room. We don't usually light it until the evenings on days when he is a work and Tom and I are at school. Fuel is in such short supply, and the Government is always asking us to save it, so Mother stays in the kitchen using the stove to keep warm by instead of having a second fire going in the sitting room as well.

Today being special, we will all sit round the fire in the sitting room. The weather doesn't invite you to go outside for a walk.

Even Tilly and Titch seem to prefer the warmth to hunting for mice in the garden, and they have found the best place on the mat in front of the fire. Titch doesn't like the fire spitting out bits of burnt wood every now and then. When a piece lands near her, she jumps up and runs for cover behind the sofa, stays there for a while, then creeps back again. Father collected some logs in the woods when he went to pick the holly. The logs are stacked beside the fireplace and will help to make the coal last longer.

The Christmas tree, standing in front of the window, looks beautiful. Every year, Mother decorates the tree on Christmas Eve after I have gone to bed. She loves doing this and she adds a few new home made decorations each year. It's a good thing that the tree keeps growing, because if it didn't grow, there wouldn't be enough room to put all the extra decorations. When Christmas is over, the tree, which is older than me, gets carried back outside in its tub and put at the end of the garden until the next Christmas comes. One day, it will become too big for Father to carry indoors.

Under the tree are our presents from Mother and Father. Tom and I put our presents for them along with the others. I wonder what they have bought us. We don't open these presents until after breakfast, so I'll have to wait a bit longer to find out.

"Breakfast is ready" Mother calls from the kitchen. It's not just Tom, Father and I who hurry to the table. Tilly and Titch, leave the fire and follow us into the kitchen, ever hopeful that a small morsel of food will find its way under the table when my parents aren't looking.

It's present time!

Mother likes the scent, which is her favourite, Lavender water. Father says the handkerchiefs will be most useful. Titch wants Tilly's bell instead of her blanket. I pull the ribbon along the floor, making the bell tinkle and they both chase after it. Round and round the room we go. Mother, Father and Tom laugh as I drag the bell up and over the back of the sofa with the cats following closely behind it. Every so often, I stop to let the cats get hold of the bell, but they start fighting about whose it is. Tilly is still the boss. She

Priscilla Winn.

hisses and smacks Titch with her paw when she wants to remind Titch of this fact.

Tom made an apron for Mother from some old material that Mrs Thomas gave him. He even embroidered a D for Dorothy, Mother's name, on the pocket. Tom and I are getting quite good at knitting and sewing. He made a lapel mascot for Miss Adams. It's a little man made of wool, fastened with a safety pin. Miss Adams was thrilled with this gift and said to the class

"This shows how we can all contrive to make use of what little is available to us in times of war. Well done Tom"

Another of her funny words, but even though I don't know what contrive means, I could tell that she was pleased, and the smirk which appeared on Joe's face when Tom handed over the present, was soon wiped away.

Father's present from Tom is a wallet made from a piece of leather. Tom broke three needles and pricked his fingers countless times trying to make the wallet.

Mother and Father thank Tom for his presents. He has worked really hard making gifts, staying up late into the night to get them finished before Christmas.

Now it's our turn. Father hands us both a present saying.

"I hope you like these and I'm sorry I couldn't get you the train set that I know you wanted William"

We open the presents and find two home made cricket bats and a cricket ball. The bats look as good as shop bought ones. I remember that Father has spent a lot of time in the shed lately, so I suppose he was making the bats in there. He's even carved our names on them.

"Thank you Father, this is super"

"Thank you Mr and Mrs Turner. It's a lovely present"

Tom and I both talk at the same time.

"It's a pity the weather is so awful today, but the first good day that we get, we'll go to the recreation ground and try them out" says Father.

There is one other present under the tree. I know who it's from

– Great Aunt Sophie. Great Aunt Sophie is Mother's aunt. She lives in Scotland. I've met her only once, just before the war started when Mother and I went by train to stay for a week.

Aunt Sophie's house is a strange place, big, dark and very old fashioned. The one thing I remember most was the horrible smell, which seemed to be everywhere. I asked Mother what the smell was and she said it was to do with Aunt Sophie's lodger, a man named Bertram Reynolds. Mr Reynolds hobby is stuffing animals and birds – taxidermy as it is called. The smell was the chemicals used for cleaning the insides of the poor creatures before they were stuffed.

Mr Reynolds is tall and thin with grey hair and glasses that perch halfway down his nose. He wears an apron that is covered in goodness knows what, to protect his clothes when he is preparing the creatures. When he looks at you, he peers over the top of the glasses. His appearance quite frightened me because I was only about five years old at the time I met him.

After saying hello, the first thing that he wanted to do was to show me all his stuffed animals. There are some in nearly every room of that house, except the kitchen and bathroom. Even the room which Mother and I slept in had a squirrel under a glass dome, preserved forever in his woodland setting, holding a nut that he would never eat. Neither Mother or I liked to gaze upon this poor little mite, so each night when we went into the room to sleep, Mother put a cover over the dome.

Great Aunt Sophie is fluffy and kindly, but she is the lady, who every year at Christmas and sometimes for my birthday as well, sends me the dreaded jigsaw puzzles. Mother says how kind it is of Aunt Sophie to think of me and that I must do the puzzle and write to say how much I enjoyed doing it, so this means that I'm always getting more of the things!

When the war started, Aunt Sophie offered Mother and I to come and stay with her, away from the bombs. She said that it would be much safer for us in the little town where her house is. Mother thanked her for the offer, but said that she could never leave Father behind, so we stayed put. Although it's been awful with all the bombing, I'm glad that we didn't go to Aunt Sophies. I'm sure that if we had, I'd be forever doing jigsaw puzzles, and if we were to go now, taking the cats with us, Mr Reynolds would probably get hold of Tilly and Titch and stick them under a glass dome. What a terrible thought!

The present is passed to me. Well' I'd better open it. With a bit of luck, I won't have to do the jigsaw for a few days.

It's NOT a jigsaw! It's a card game called "Belisha" Perhaps Aunt Sophie has bought every picture of jigsaw puzzle available in the small town where she lives and now has to find other presents for me. Hooray.

I'm looking forward to playing Belisha. There's a knock on the front door and Mother goes to see who it is. I can hear voices in the hall, then Mrs Thomas comes into the room carrying a large cardboard box.

"Merry Christmas everyone" she says and we return the greeting.

"This box is very heavy, could you boys help me with it please" she asks.

Tom and I get up off the floor, where we have been laying the "Belisha" cards out to look at, take the box from Mrs Thomas and put it on the table.

"Go on then, open it" she says.

Wondering whatever can be in the box, I lift the lid, and when Tom and I look inside, we can see a tin train, carriages, station building, tunnel and lots of railway track. It's the same set as the one I saw in the toyshop window. The man who owns the shop had the train set laid out and running. It was a beautiful model, just like a real train. I stood for ages, watching the train, wishing that I could have one, and then the man must have noticed my face pressed against the window, for he came outside and said that I could have a go at running the train if I wanted to. Of course I said yes. It was great fun. The man told me that the train belonged to him when he was a boy. "Most boys your age want train sets, but it's very difficult to get them at the moment. I thought that if I put my old one in the window, you could at least see the train even if I can't offer it for sale. I've promised it to my little grandson when he is old enough to play with it" he said.

Mrs Thomas is talking

"Stan was in the spare room the other day, getting the decorations out of the cupboard and he found Frank's train set. We had forgotten that it was there, Frank being all grown up now. I said to Stan, I know two boys who would like this, so he tested the train to see if it still works, cos it hasn't been used for years, and would you believe, it goes a treat"

"That's most kind of you. Are you sure that you don't mind the boys playing with it" says Mother.

"If Frank were here, I know that he would be pleased to let William and Tom have his train" says Mrs Thomas, and her usually jolly face suddenly looks sad. She takes a handkerchief out of her pocket and starts to wipe a tear from her eye.

"It's alright. Don't mind me, I'm just being silly. Frank was due to have leave for Christmas because the war was going so well. We haven't seen him for ages and I was so excited about him coming home, but then we heard that there's been a German counter attack in the Ardennes and his leave has been cancelled. Frank sent us a card and lovely presents, but it's not the same as having him here with us"

We all say how sorry we are to hear this news. What a disappointment this must be for Mr and Mrs Thomas.

"Why don't you come and spend Christmas with us" says Mother. I think what a good idea this is. Surely we can cheer Mrs Thomas up a bit. It's got to be better than Mr Thomas and her being all on their own next door.

"That would be nice. Stan's as upset as I am about Frank not getting home. We'd planned to give him a real traditional Christmas – well as much as we could manage under the circumstances. I made a Christmas cake and a trifle. That's Frank's favourite is trifle, got a bit of sherry in it from an old bottle I found in the back of the larder. I'll bring the food over when we come"

Mother shows Mrs Thomas out, then says to Tom and me

"Come on boys. You can help peel some more vegetables to go with the dinner. There's plenty from the garden to feed six people"

The vegetables are done and dinner isn't for another two hours. I'd like to get the train running and to play a game of "Belisha", but I'd also like to give Mr and Mrs Thomas a happy day. I decide to try to make crackers to have with the dinner. We've got some old wallpaper, which might be suitable for the crackers, and Tom knows lots of jokes that we could write on pieces of paper. There's even a few sweets left over from the rations to put inside the crackers.

I tell Tom my idea and we go to fetch all the things that we will need. It's a pity we haven't got anything to make the bang when the cracker breaks, but we can always say "BANG" instead.

It takes an hour to make six crackers and they don't look too bad when finished. We've even managed to cut out little hats from some old paper bags and decorated them with paint.

Mr and Mrs Thomas arrive with their cake and trifle. Mrs Thomas is a good cook so the cake and trifle are bound to taste delicious.

Although the weathers not improved outside, it's lovely and warm in the sitting room, with the logs burning brightly in the fireplace. There haven't been any air raids so far today, and everyone's hoping that at least, just for this one day, we will be left in peace to enjoy our celebrations. I overheard Mrs Thomas telling Mother and Father there was a report on the radio, that yesterday, 50 Heinkel aircraft, each carrying a doodlebug, crossed the coast between Skegness and Mablethorpe, launching their V1's towards Manchester. Thankfully, not all of the bombs hit targets, but the worst place to be hit was Oldham where 32 people were killed and 49 badly injured.

Mr Thomas accepts Fathers offer of a seat by the fire. He has brought his slippers with him to be more comfortable and he settles down with his legs outstretched towards the warmth.

Unfortunately, Titch has other ideas. Suddenly, she springs upon poor Mr Thomas, slides down his trouser leg and clings onto his slipper, kicking it with her back feet. It's a great game to her, but Mr Thomas doesn't think so. He tries to shake her off with no success and eventually, I have to go and remove her from his foot.

Our dining table is really meant for only four people, but we have all managed to squeeze in somehow. Mrs Thomas and Mother bring the food through from the kitchen on a trolley. There are roast potatoes, carrots, brussel sprouts and murkey with stuffing. The stuffing is made from grated carrots, breadcrumbs, margarine, grated nutmeg, ginger and dried egg mixed together with milk and water. The recipe says add a teaspoon of sultanas but we couldn't get any of these. Thick brown "Bisto" gravy poured over the dinner gives it a nice taste.

There is never a plate with food left over. Rations means that most days we are still hungry after our meals because there isn't enough food to go round. But, after eating Christmas dinner, followed by Mother's pudding with mock cream and Mrs Thomas's trifle, I feel really full up.

The crackers are popular, although it's not easy to pull them. I think that the wallpaper is too thick to break easily. Everyone is wearing their paper hats and Tom's jokes make us laugh. Here are some of them.

Question	Why are Christmas trees like bad knitters?
Answer	They both drop their needles.
Q	What happens to you at Christmas?
A	Yule be happy.
Q	What's Christmas called in England?
A	Yule Britannia.
Q	What do you get if you cross an apple with a Christmas tree?
A	A pineapple.

Priscilla Winn.

Q   Why can you never play jokes on snakes?
A   You can never pull their legs.

Diner   Waiter, waiter, my Christmas pudding if off.
Waiter   Off, where to?

Tom and I start to do the washing up like we promised, while the grown ups sit round the fire listening to the radio. To make the washing up less boring, we have a fight with the soapsuds. Tom puts a handful down my back and I flick the dishcloth at him sending suds all over his face. It's good fun. When we've finished washing all the dishes and have wiped up most of the suds that landed on the floor, we creep back into the sitting room a bit wet but no one notices. Mr Thomas is taking a nap, Father is reading a book and Mother and Mrs Thomas are waiting for the King's speech to come on the radio.

Mrs Thomas nudges Mr Thomas, who is snoring loudly with the paper hat still on his head.

"Stan, the King's speech is about to start"

Mr Thomas wakes up, quickly takes the paper hat off his head, straightens his tie and strokes his hair down. Mrs Thomas arranges her skirt tidily on the sofa, and fluffs her hair up. Then, they both sit upright waiting. You'd think that the King was going to walk into the sitting room.

Father lays his book down. All the grown ups want to hear what the King has to say and I know that I'm expected to be quiet whilst the broadcast is on.

The message goes on a bit and ends with this

"The defeat of Germany and Japan is only the first half of our task; the second is to create a world of free men "untouched by tyranny". I wish you, from my heart, a happy Christmas, and, for the coming year, a full measure of that courage and faith in God which alone enables us to bear old sorrows and face new trials, until the day when the Christmas message – peace on earth and goodwill towards men – finally comes true"

Mrs Thomas says how she admires the King and Queen, supporting their people by staying in London during the bombing and visiting bombed areas.

"Why, the poor souls were even bombed themselves in the blitz of 1940" she says.

Father mentions he heard that King George VI and Queen Elizabeth go in an armoured car each evening to Windsor Castle to avoid the night raids.

A quiz comes on the radio, which interests Mother and Mrs Thomas. It's all about food.

What is the correct way of mixing milk powder?

How much is fresh salted cod per pound?

Which vitamins does cod liver oil contain?

What is/are rose hips? 1 A dress design 2 An authoress 3 An Eastern dance 4 Pods of wild roses rich in Vitamin C

They know all the answers.

Mr Thomas has gone back to sleep again. Mother and Mrs Thomas keep on with the quiz and Father goes to bring in some more logs from the shed to put on the fire. Tom and I find a nice big space in a corner of the room to lay out the train set.

Despite the disappointments of Tom not hearing from his Father and Frank Thomas's leave being cancelled, we are all trying to make the best of Christmas, and it's not going too badly.

The train set was a great surprise for Tom and me. We spent the whole afternoon playing with it, changing the layout of the track every so often. At present, the track winds its way around two chair legs, through the tunnel, goes past the station and then goes through another tunnel that we made out of books stacked on top of each other. Tom's tin whistle comes in handy when we take it in turns to be the guard.

Mrs Thomas's Battenberg cake, which we had at tea-time, was a great success. The two coloured sponge with jam filling and vanilla flavoured coating was delicious.

Mother and Mr and Mrs Thomas are listening to "Christmas Night at Eight" on the radio. There's a comedy "Christmas at

Much Binding in the Marsh" with Arthur Askey, Richard Murdoch and Kenneth Horne, on at the moment. Mrs Thomas is enjoying the programme. She laughs louder than both Mother and Mr Thomas put together.

Tilly and Titch stretch out side by side in front of the fire. I got told to put the bell away because, as I thought, the noise got on everyone's (not Toms) nerves, but the cats had a lot of fun playing with it and now they are tired from running round the room and up and down the stairs behind me and the bell.

I ask Father if he would like to play Great Aunt Sophie's card game "Belisha" with Tom and me. He says yes, so we leave the others listening to the programme and go into the kitchen to use the table for the game. Apparently, "Belisha" is named after the Belisha Beacon which was introduced at Zebra crossings in 1934. There are 52 brightly coloured cards plus a joker, which show places of interest in Britain from London to Oban in Scotland. There is a number and a road sign at the top left hand corner of each card. Some of the cards are quite funny – one has a couple stuck in the middle of a big puddle in their car and another shows a man reading a newspaper whilst crossing a road, while the joker shows a Scotsman dressed in tartan with a tartan coloured car that has a registration number OCH I.

It says in the rule book "Belisha has been produced with a sincere desire to make a helpful contribution to the "Safety First" Campaign. It has been carefully designed to stimulate road consciousness, especially amongst young people"

We soon get the hang of playing "Belisha" It's fun. You have to add up the numbers on the cards and the game ends when a player has a score of 250 or more. When I write my thank you letter to Great Aunt Sophie, saying how much I enjoyed her present, I will really mean it this time.

12 Tom, Father and I are in the recreation ground. It's Boxing Day, freezing cold and we are trying out the cricket bats Father made for us. I couldn't wait for the weather to improve and I've managed to persuade Father to take us here today. He says that most sensible people are staying indoors and that seems to be the case because we haven't seen a soul since we've been here.

Holding my bat in gloved hands, I try to keep my eyes on the ball that Father is bowling to me. The fog certainly doesn't help much, and we are spending a lot of time hunting for the ball after we've hit it as it just disappears into the gloom. The bats work well and Father looks pleased that we are happy with them.

Tom and I take turns at batting whilst Father does the bowling. Tom's much better than I am at hitting the ball. He really whacks it hard and I have to run a long distance to search for it in the frozen grass. All this chasing around is warming me up, but my nose won't stop running. I can't keep stopping to get my handkerchief out of my pocket and field at the same time, so I just wipe my nose on the sleeve of my coat. Father would tell me off if he saw me doing this. It would seem to me to be a good idea if I was to pin a handkerchief to the back of my sleeve, but I still think that Father would complain.

On the way back home, we find a frozen puddle. I can't resist sliding over it and Tom copies me. It's great fun, except when you slip over and bump your bottom!

Priscilla Winn.

"Come on Father. You have a go" I say, and, to my surprise, Father puts his foot on the puddle and slides over just as if he was a boy again. He must have liked it, because, even more surprisingly, he goes and does it a second time. Mother will wish that she had been with us to see this when I tell her.

13

The day after Boxing Day, we heard on the radio that the Germans had started bombing again. The first of the bombs landed at Nazeing, just after 9 p.m. on Boxing Day evening. At 9.20 p.m. "The Price of Wales" public house in Islington, London, had a bomb land on it. The Announcer on the radio said "The pub was very full with people celebrating Christmas and, because of this, 68 people lost their lives"

On New Years Eve, Tom and I were allowed to stay up to see the New Year in. We were in the sitting room listening to the radio. Mother wanted to hear the BBC broadcast of the midnight service at St Paul's Cathedral. Suddenly, the choir stopped singing for a few minutes, then started again. Apparently, a bomb exploded nearby and blew out the last of the Cathedrals remaining windows.

Now, it's 1945, the sixth year of the war, and nobody seems to know how much longer it will go on. One good thing – Tom has heard from his Father. A letter came a week ago. Tom showed me what his Father had written. Mr Finch said that he was well and Tom needn't worry about him. He asked Tom to thank my parents for taking such good care of him. It was a great comfort to know Tom was being well cared for by such kind people. He looked forward to meeting Mr and Mrs Turner and William when the war is over.

Mother has decided that we all need a holiday. Not the usual sort where you go and stay in a different place. We haven't had one of those holidays since the war started. Because of the fuel shortage, the Government has advised us not to make journeys that aren't necessary. Their latest idea is that we have "Holidays at home" - A day out to somewhere nearby on foot or a picnic in the garden if the weather's good.

Mother's plan is for us to go to Chislehurst Common. The Common starts about a mile from where we live. I thought that the Common was just all woods, but Mother says that there are pathways, which lead to fields and there is even a little pond with frogs and fish in it. Also, at the end of Watts Lane on the edge of the Common, is a proper cricket ground with a pavilion where we can have a picnic on the veranda because it's too early in the year to sit on the damp grass.

This sounds like a great day. I'd love a chance to use the cricket bats on a real cricket ground and I can take my fishing net and a jam jar to try to catch some fish to look at.

"When can we go?" Tom asks the question that is on the tip of my tongue.

"The first week end day that shows dry weather. We can't really expect a heat wave at this time of year, but as long as it's dry and bright, it should be alright to go" says Mother.

Today is Wednesday. We had a bit of rain this morning and it rained yesterday as well. I hope all the rain comes over the next two days, then we might be lucky on Saturday and have our "Holiday at Home" I'm going to find my fishing net which I think is somewhere in the shed and ask Mother for a jam jar.

14

"William. What is there outside the window that is so interesting? Perhaps you could kindly share this information with the rest of the class"

Miss Adams has caught me staring at the rain, which is falling on the playground. It's been raining for an hour now. I've timed it by the clock on the wall behind her desk.

Going red in the face, I mumble.

"Sorry Miss. I was just watching the rain" and turn back to the sums she has set us to do.

At the end of the lesson, which is the last one of the day, I decide to ask Miss Adams if she knows what the weather might be like on Saturday and Sunday. Miss Adams knows the answers to most things.

"The weather forecasts aren't always accurate, so you can't be completely sure, but, according to my newspaper, tomorrow should be a little better than today" she says.

Tomorrow is Saturday, the day we may or may not be having our "Holiday at home"

"Did your paper say it will rain?" I ask

"There is a chance of rain, but probably not as much as today"

"Oh" The weather doesn't sound as if it's going to be much good for our outing.

"Why are you so concerned about the weather William?" asks Miss Adams.

"We are going to have a day out to Chislehurst Common. Mother knows where there is a pond with fish in it and then we are going to play cricket at the cricket ground in Watts Lane. We may go tomorrow, but not if the weather stays rainy" I say.

"Well, I hope that it brightens up for you. I have something that might be useful when you visit the pond." Miss Adams goes over to her bookcase and takes a small book from one of the shelves.

"This is a pocket book on pond life. It tells you about the creatures that live in ponds and it has illustrations to help you identify them. I found it most useful when I was a girl"

I can't imagine Miss Adams, who is so tidy and beautifully dressed, as a young girl, poking around in ponds, picking up frogs and insects. Most of the girls I know would run a mile if I were to show them a frog, and they certainly wouldn't want to hold one!

Taking the book, I thank her and put it in my satchel.

"Off you go now, and have a lovely time if you manage to get to the Common over the week end" Miss Adams starts to tidy her desk, ready for when we return to school on Monday morning.

"Wow ! Look at that. Let's hope we find one of them" Tom points to a picture in Miss Adams's book of a great diving beetle.

We both read

The beetle has broad hairy back legs, which it beats to push itself through the water. It is a fierce hunter that will attack almost anything that comes within its reach, including creatures much larger than itself, such as frogs and sticklebacks. Diving beetles are sometimes known as water tigers. They use their large jaws to tear up the food they catch. If the pond that the beetle is living in becomes too crowded, it can move to another pond because it is a strong flier, usually flying at night.

"Sounds revolting" says Mother when we tell her about the beetle. Why can't you just be content with catching sticklebacks. I think they are rather sweet"

"Oh, we want to find sticklebacks as well Mrs Turner" replies Tom, then goes on to say "Did you know that in springtime, the male stickleback turns bright red so that he can attract a female. When he finds one, he dances in front of her showing off his red belly. It's all in this little book"

"How interesting" says Mother, looking a bit embarrassed.

It has finally stopped raining and now it's getting dark. Tom and I have got everything ready for tomorrow, just in case we are able to get to the pond. The fishing net, jam jar, Miss Adams's book, magnifying glass (borrowed from Father) cricket bats and ball, plus a notebook and pencil to make a list of what we find, are stacked in a heap in our bedroom. Father will also insist that we take our gas masks, so I've put them with everything else.

Mother has cleaned the old picnic hamper, which hasn't been used for ages, ready to put our food in. Now, all we need is the sunshine.

15   Last night, I set my alarm clock for 7 a.m. The shrill ringing of it, wakes me up.

The alarm doesn't wake Tom, who seems to be able to sleep through any noise. Even Tilly and Titch are still asleep in their baskets. I get out of bed, forget to put my slippers on and tip toe over the cold linoleum floor to the window. I want to see what the weathers like. It's just starting to get light, but it's still too early to tell if it's going to be sunny or not. I open the window and stretch my hand outside, palm upwards. Can't feel any rain.

Mother is bound to be up by now. I put on my dressing gown and go downstairs to the kitchen.

"Hello William, You're up early" she says.

"I wanted to see what the weather was like" I reply.

"We won't be going for another couple of hours. If it's still not raining by then, I think that it will be alright to have our outing. I was just about to start making some sandwiches, so you might as well give me a hand"

Mother opens a tin of corned beef to put in the sandwiches and then gets a jar of home made chutney out of the cupboard.

Tilly and Titch have woken up, and rush through the door meowing loudly. I'm sure that they have some sense which tells them when we are opening tins of corned beef, because they always seem to appear at this moment, corned beef being one of their favourite things.

I cut the meat into thin slices. The tin has got to last us for two days. Tomorrow we will probably have corned beef fritters with what's left over. The cats sit looking hopefully up at me, their noses twitching with the smell of the meat. I drop tiny pieces onto the floor, and they both rush to get it. Titch is much more determined now to have her share of any treats, and I've seen Tilly back away sometimes when she won't give in to her.

Mother fills a thermos flask with tea, saying "It's much better to take a hot drink for all of us. You'll need it, after fishing round in that cold pond William"

Also, for the picnic, we have some spicy buns and a swiss roll.

The picnic hamper is packed. Father and Tom come down for breakfast. Outside, it's not raining and there is even a bit of blue sky.

16

We are on the Common, walking along a path that runs beside the railway line. You can only see the line when you look over the fence on your left, because it lies in a cutting. This line goes up to London.

There's more blue sky now and the sun is coming out. Mother made us put on thick jumpers and waterproof coats, just in case the weather changes, but there's no sign of rain yet, and it's even getting quite warm.

Birds are chirping in the trees, which are mostly oaks and silver birches, plus a few other types of tree that I don't know the names of. I've seen three squirrels already – two high up in the trees and another ran across the path right in front of us.

Tom and I are carrying the hamper to give Father a rest. He's got our bats and ball, net, jam jar and gas masks. Mother carries a rug to spread on the pavilion's wooden seat for when we have our picnic. She thinks the wood might still be wet and cold. I wouldn't have minded a bit of damp wood, but Mother says there's no need to be uncomfortable.

Further along the path, we come to a place where another path joins it. I've never been here before, but my parents know the way.

We take the other path and keep going until a field appears on the left. The path carries on to the end of the field, then turns left and goes down another side of the field. At the next corner, Mother leads us off the path through a wood where there is no path. We step over a tangle of small blackberry bushes that catch against our trouser legs, then, there it is in front of us, a hidden pond. What a super place.

The pond is green in colour. Most of the water is covered with algae, which is a tiny plant that has no leaves, roots or flowers. I've been reading Miss Adams's book, so that's why I know what it is.

"Look" says Tom, pointing to something in the water. A young tree has fallen down across the pond. The algae has covered parts of the trunk, but the other bits that rise above the water, look like the back of a crocodile, lying in the water. There is even a bit of knotted trunk at the end that is just like a crocodile's face with two bumpy eyes and a pointed nose.

"Good job it's not a real one" says Father.

Mother finds a large tree trunk and spreads the rug on it for she and Father to sit on, whilst Tom and I explore the pond.

"I'm not sure how deep the water is, so take care when you are fishing. We don't want you ending up in the pond" she says.

I notice a bit of water where the algae, is not growing. It seems the best spot to start fishing. Tom has the jam jar, magnifying glass, notebook and pencil and I've got the net. While I dip the net into the pond, he fills the jam jar with water ready to put anything we might catch in it.

The pond isn't very clear and the first time that I take the net out of the water, all I can see in it is some rotten leaves and mud which smell rather horrible. I rinse the net and decide not to put it right down to the bottom of the pond next time. The water is only about a foot deep here so I drag the net along making sure to keep it just below the surface. This time, I'm in luck, a snail is caught in the net.

I gently tip the snail into the jam jar. Tom gets the book out of his pocket and looks up snails. We both agree that it's a great pond snail or lymnaea stagnalis, as the book says its fancy name is. Pond snails live in water containing a lot of chalk. I remember Miss Adams telling us that this part of Kent is very chalky, so I suppose that's why we've found one here.

Tom writes "pond snail" in our notebook. Then we have a look at it through the magnifying glass. It's a funny creature. The book says that the snail's head is at one end of its foot. How strange. It also says that the snail's shell is made from chalk. As its body grows, it makes its shell grow bigger too.

Before we put the snail back into the water, we show it to Mother and Father. Then Tom has a turn with the net. He doesn't find anything, so we move along the pond to another place. The sun is shining on this part of the pond, and I can see small fish moving in the water. Toms seen them too, and he slowly dips the net in behind the fish and moves it towards them. The fish start to swim off. Perhaps they can see us above them. Tom takes a chance and quickly sweeps the net through the water, then lifts it out. Would you believe it, he's got one! The tiny fish is wriggling in the net.

"Let's get it in the jam jar" says Tom, looking very excited.

When the fish is safely in the jar, we look closely at it. There are three spiky bits on its back and its body is red.

"A male stickleback. Your Mother will want to see this" Tom proudly carries the fish over to Mother.

We spend about an hour fishing in the pond, finding one more stickleback, lots more snails, water boatmen, which are a kind of water bug and a frog that was impossible to catch because it swam out of our reach. We don't manage to find the great diving beetle.

Mother calls us to say it's time to move on to the cricket ground for our picnic. I'd quite happily stay here all day, but I'm also getting rather hungry and am looking forward to playing cricket.

Gathering up all our belongings, we go back to the path and carry along it until we get to a farm track. The track leads to a lane called Hawkwood Lane. At the end of Hawkwood Lane, we turn left, then we are in Watts Lane. It's only a short walk before we come to the cricket ground.

The pavilion is like a little bungalow made of wood with a tiled roof. Although the doors are locked so we can't go inside, there is a veranda at the front with a wooden seat. Just right for our picnic. Mother starts to get everything out of the hamper.

My hands are very dirty from being in and out of the pond. So are Toms. Mother says to go and wash them, there is a tap round the side of the pavilion.

We've just finished washing our hands and are wiping them dry on our trousers, when I hear a whining noise. Looking up, I see what I think is one of our spitfire planes in the sky, some distance away, heading in this direction. Then, Father and Mother come running round the corner of the pavilion and Father says "Quick boys, stop what you are doing and run!"

17 It's not a spitfire, it's a doodlebug!

We are running as fast as we can across the cricket ground, with the whining sound behind us getting louder all the time. Father is shouting "We must get to the caves over the road"

Chislehurst Caves is a public air raid shelter. Other people have seen the doodlebug and are running like us in the direction of the caves. The air raid sirens are going off.

There are two cars coming along the road and we have to wait before we can cross it. The first driver refuses to stop. He seems to be trying to speed away from the bomb. I look back and see the doodlebug is getting closer. Then, Father says "run!" and pushes Tom and me into the road. The driver of the second car hoots his horn at us as we run in front of him, but we make it to the other side and now the caves are right in front of us.

We all rush through the narrow entrance into the caves. Father leans against the chalky wall of the cave, coughing and trying to breathe properly. His damaged lungs must have found it difficult to cope with running so fast.

"I'll be alright in a minute" he says.

We are all shaking and out of breath, and my heart is beating so fast, that I'm wondering if it's ever going to slow down.

"That was a close one" says Tom, and Mother looks as white as a sheet.

There's no sound of an explosion. I don't know if you'd be able to hear it from inside the caves. Father says that the doodlebug may have passed over on its way to London. Tower Bridge is supposed to be the fixed target for the doodlebugs, but sometimes they fall to earth before reaching the target. If the Anti – aircraft guns miss any of the doodlebugs, then our Spitfire, Hurricane and Typhoon pilots go up and try to tip the wings on the doodlebug to bring it down over open land.

"Unfortunately, this doodlebug is now over houses and our pilots are given instructions not to intercept them over populated areas" he says.

We are all quiet for a while and I expect that Mother, Father and Tom are thinking the same awful thought as I am – how many more people will be killed or injured by the doodlebug.

Mother is the first to speak again

"I could do with a cup of tea" she says "Perhaps we can find a biscuit too. Come on boys, there's a stand over there where we can get some. It will warm us up a bit" She's trying to be cheery for Toms and my sake, but her hands are still shaking as she tries to take her purse out of her pocket.

Besides us, there's only one other person in this part of the caves. An old man is sitting on a fold up chair beside the tea urn. The people whom we saw running into the caves must have gone further inside. Mother says that there are over 20 miles of caverns and that mushrooms used to be grown here before the war started.

"Been another of them doodlebugs gone over has there?" asks the old man.

"Yes" replies Father.

"I was already in here. Well, to tell the truth, Annie and I spend most of our time here now" says the old man. He leans over and strokes the back of a small white dog, which is lying by his feet.

"Do you have a home nearby?" asks Mother.

"Oh yes. It's just down the road, but it doesn't feel like home anymore, so I come here instead. In the evenings when the London folk arrive to spend the night in the caves, it's very busy and I enjoy the company"

"You live alone then, do you?" asks Father.

"Yes, I lost my dear wife Elsie last year. She went out to the shops- said she was going to try to get a nice piece of salted cod for my tea, and that was the last I saw of her. Next thing I knew, someone came to the door to tell me a bomb had landed in the High Street and she'd been killed. I couldn't believe it at first. We'd been together for nearly forty years and I didn't even get a chance to say goodbye to her."

We all say how sorry we are to hear this. The poor old man must be so lonely without his wife.

I'm shivering. It's quite cold in here and I wish that I had my coat on. Tom and I left our coats on the seat in the pavilion. We were feeling warm after our walk from the pond, so we took them off.

Mother is looking for cups to put the tea in but there aren't any.

"Here, I've got a couple of spare cups you can use" says the old man, and he picks up a large bag which is on the floor and gets two tea cups out of it.

"That's very kind of you" says Mother, taking the cups and filling them with tea.

"Got a few sweets the boys would probably like" He rummages around in the bag and brings out a bag of toffees.

"Can you spare them?" asks Mother.

"Yes, take a handful, boys"

The old man says that his name is Albert Clark. We introduce ourselves and Tom tells him about what we were doing before we ended up in the caves.

"Used to fish in that pond myself when I was a boy. I fell in once and got soaked. My mum gave me a right telling off when I got home" says Albert.

Chewing a toffee and drinking tea at the same time isn't easy to do. I have to make sure that the toffee is stuck to some of my teeth before I swallow a mouthful of the tea.

Father is still coughing every now and then.

"Nasty cough you've got there" says Albert "There's a nurse down here who comes round with cough mixture for a penny a spoonful"

"I'm afraid cough mixture won't help much. I've got damaged lungs from the First World War" replies Father.

"You poor devil. Wouldn't you think they'd learnt something from that atrocity to ever want to start another one" says Albert.

"Want a game of darts boys?" he asks, pointing to a dartboard fixed to the cave wall. There is an electric light above the board so you can see where to throw the darts.

"Used to be just candlelight in here at the beginning of the war, but now we're all modern. Would you believe there's three canteens, a dance floor, one of them gymnasium things, cinema, hospital and a chapel down here – a regular little city all underground. I've got my own bunk to sleep in – costs me sixpence a week. Children go free. They even let me take Annie in with me"

Albert is really good at darts. I'm just pleased if my dart gets anywhere on the board, because, mostly, it seems to bounce off it and fall on the floor. Tom's not much better, but we're enjoying the game and starting to feel a little warmer.

While Albert, Tom and I are playing darts, or in Toms and my case, trying to play darts, Mother and Father have gone to see if they can get anything for us to eat from the canteen. Breakfast seems a long while ago, and we are getting very hungry. Father said that it would be best to stay in the caves a little longer because there could be more doodlebugs coming this way.

Albert teaches us how to hold the darts, and I'm beginning to get a bit better, when Mother and Father return with a plate of bread and dripping and a few plain biscuits. Not as nice as the corned beef sandwiches, swiss roll and the buns that we were going to have, but that's all there is. I'm not fond of bread and dripping, but I've learnt that if there's nothing else and you're hungry, you just have to put up with it and eat it.

We share the food with Albert and even little Annie gets a bit of bread and dripping. She's a really friendly dog and Albert shows us how he has taught her to hold her paw up and shake our hands.

After we have eaten, Father looks at his watch.

"I'll go and see if the "All Clear" siren has gone off. If so, we should be getting home once we have collected our things. There's a bus which runs back to Petts Wood that we can catch" he says

Mother has written down our address on a piece of paper and she gives it to Albert saying

"Perhaps you would like to come for lunch next weekend. Harold could meet you at the bus stop"

"That would be very nice, but, if you don't mind, I'll have to bring Annie with me. She's all I've got now and I don't let her out of my sight"

"Of course you can bring her" says Mother.

It's arranged that Albert and Annie will come for lunch on Sunday of next weekend. Goodness knows what Tilly and Titch will make of Annie.

Father comes back saying that the "All Clear" siren has gone off, so we all say goodbye to Albert and leave the caves.

Although the siren has gone off, I can't help wondering if there will be any more bombs coming over before we get home. It's beginning to rain as we cross the road and start to walk across the cricket ground towards the pavilion.

When we get there, we can't believe what we find, or rather don't find waiting for us. The hamper and food, which Mother had laid out, rug, cricket bats, ball and both Tom's and my coats are gone! All that's left are the gas masks, fishing net and jam jar.

Whilst we've been in the caves, someone must have stolen our belongings. What a rotten thing to do.

"Oh dear" says Mother, and Father goes a bit further and utters a swear word, which is most unlike him because he never swears.

The rain is getting worse, and this only seems to make us even more miserable.

"Let's get home as quickly as possible" says Mother, picking up the gas masks, net and jam jar.

We shelter under a big old tree that is growing on the green next to the bus stop, and have to wait for twenty minutes before a bus comes along.

Once home, we change out of our wet clothes, then Mother says

"I think that I've got some of those spicy buns left in the larder. Who wants one and a cup of cocoa?"

18 I'm really upset about losing my cricket bat. Father had spent so much time making the bats for us, and we had only used them once on Boxing Day.

Tom and I are standing by Miss Adams's desk. It's the end of the school day, and we are waiting to return her pond life book. It wasn't stolen because Tom had it in his trouser pocket, but it's not in as good condition as it was when she lent it to us. The rain soaked the book as well as our clothes, and although I tried to dry it in front of the fire when I got home, some of the pages went a bit crinkly.

Miss Adams looks up from her desk, sees us and asks

"Did you have your day out at the week end William?"

I tell her all about Saturday and when I've finished, Tom shows her the bedraggled book.

Miss Adams examines the book and says

"It's disappointing, but you must remember that this is only a book, and there are much more important things in life. Of course you should never steal other peoples' possessions (Tom is going red – he still feels guilty about trying to loot that bombed house) but, I have noticed that the war has changed some people, making them behave in a way that they might not have done under other circumstances. Having to go without so many everyday things that before the war we used to take for granted, must make it very tempting for some people to just help themselves to anything they might find lying around."

Then she says

"I have also noticed that, because of the war, some people have become more thoughtful of others - not always thinking of themselves, and this is good. It seems to me that your day wasn't a complete waste. You have made a new friend in Albert, a man who has suffered a great loss and who is in need of support and companionship, which I am sure that your family will offer him"

Walking home from school, I think about what Miss Adams said. She's right, losing my cricket bat is nothing compared to what Albert has lost.

19 Tom and I have been hearing these really loud noises in the sky. The noise hurts our ears and sounds like a thunderclap, followed by a roaring sound. We hear if quite often, and the other day I asked Father what the noise was. He said it's probably gas main explosions caused by bombs.

At school today, we are in the playground talking to some of the boys in our class and someone mentions the noise.

"My Father says it's probably gas main explosions" I say.

"No it's not. This is what it is" one of the boys hands me a newspaper cutting.

Tom leans over my shoulder so that he can read what is written.

The V2 Rocket comes to Southern England

The most indiscriminate weapon of this or any other war – a sinister eerie form of war. Britains front line at home is under fire again from a stratospheric rocket that is dropping on us from 60 to 70 miles up in the air, a rocket that travels faster than sound and flashes across the sky like a comet trailing fire. There is no siren warning, no time to take shelter.

I don't know what indiscriminate or stratospheric mean, but the rest of the newspaper story makes the rocket sound much worse even than the doodlebug.

"That's terrible. How could anyone invent such a thing" says Tom.

"Pity we didn't invent it first" says Joe, who has pushed his way into our conversation and has been looking over my other shoulder to read the story.

"I wonder if I should tell Father about the rockets?" I ask Tom, when the other boys have gone off to play their war games.

"I think that he already knows. Your Father takes the same newspaper that the story was printed in and he always reads the newspaper from cover to cover, so he must have seen it. I expect that he thinks it's better for us not to know about the rockets" says Tom.

We both agree that it would probably only upset Father if we told him that we have found out what the noise in the sky is.

20 I looked in Father's newspaper which he left behind when he went to work, and read that over twenty V2 rockets fell last week. In the paper it says "A single V2 can cause a crater as large as 50 feet wide and 10 feet deep. The incredibly loud double bang that heralds each V2 can make people up to ten miles away think that it is about to fall on them." I suppose that when Tom and I hear the rocket, it must be no more than ten miles from us. It also says in the paper that bombs have fallen in Bromley, Chislehurst and Orpington, which are all near where we live.

Although, my parents never mention the rockets, Mother has taken to walking with us to school and meeting us at the end of the afternoon. Once, we heard the rocket on the way home and I saw the worried look on Mother's face as she hurried us along the road. We have got so used to running into air raid shelters when bombs are coming over, but with this new bomb it's different. It comes out of nowhere and shoots through the air so fast that nothing can stop it.

Albert and Annie visit us every weekend. The first time that they were coming, Mother told me to shut Tilly and Titch in my bedroom in case they picked a fight with Annie. Tilly and Titch didn't much like being shut in. They scratched the door and cried to be let out. When Annie arrived, she put her nose in the air and sniffed, then she went round the house looking for the cats. She soon found where Tilly and Titch were and stood outside my bedroom door barking. To get her to come away, I had to coax her downstairs with a bone. Annie loves bones. Mother had queued for ages at the butcher's shop for some meat and she managed to get four ox tails to put in a stew with dumplings. Annie's bone had been used to make soup with before we gave it to her. Because of all the food shortages, the bits of meat called offal, that were usually thrown away, are now eaten and sometimes when you have queued for a long time at the butchers, that's all there is left.

Annie settled down underneath the kitchen table chewing her bone, whilst we ate our lunch. Albert said how tasty the stew was, and then he told us that when he was a boy, he had eight brothers and sisters. "We were a poor family, with all those kids. My mum often used to get pig's trotters and sheep's heads from the butcher to feed us all on" he said.

After our meal, Tom and I did the washing up while Mother, Father and Albert sat around the table talking. None of us had noticed that Annie had sneaked out of the room. Albert was the first to see that she was missing. "She's probably off looking for the cats again" said Mother.

I went into the hall and up the stairs, thinking to find her outside my bedroom door, but she wasn't there. Then, Tom called me from downstairs.

"William, look at this!"

If I hadn't have seen it with my own eyes, I wouldn't have believed it. On the mat in front of the fireplace, lying fast asleep were Annie, Tilly and Titch!

"Well, I'll be blowed!" said Albert when we showed him.

It was a mystery how Tilly and Titch had managed to escape from the bedroom. The door was still shut and no one had gone into the room since Albert and Annie arrived, so they must have got out some other way.

"Perhaps they climbed up the chimney and went down the roof" said Tom, looking up the chimney.

"It seems rather impossible, but I wouldn't put anything past those cats" said Father.

Then, I noticed that the top of one of the bedroom windows was open. It was just about wide enough for Tilly and Titch to squeeze through. I went downstairs and found the window in the sitting room was also open.

"I think that they may have squeezed through the bedroom window, slid down the wall and then got in through the sitting room window" I said.

"We'll never know for sure, but whichever way they escaped, I'm sure that they must have used up one of the "nine lives" that cats are supposed to be blessed with" said Mother.

It was amazing how well Tilly and Titch got along with Annie. We had all thought that there would be a terrible fight if they were to meet each other, but instead they have become good friends. I've even seen Tilly washing Annie's face with her tongue. Just amazing!

21

Amazing and unexpected things do happen.

We have lived for weeks with the awful V2 rockets still coming over, then, this morning, at breakfast, Mother told Tom and me, that last night at 10.30pm, when she was listening to the BBC Home Service on the radio, the programme was interrupted by a news flash. This is what the announcer said:

"This is London Calling. Here is a news flash. The German radio has just announced that Hitler is dead. I repeat, the German radio has just announced that Hitler is dead"

Nothing else was said. The "Evening Prayers" programme followed immediately after the announcement.

"Does this mean that the war is over?" I ask, hardly believing what she has said.

"It would seem very likely that the war will come to an end now, although the Prime Minister hasn't made an announcement yet"

Tom's first question is "My Father will be home soon won't he?"

"I hope so" says Mother.

I still can't believe what Mother has told us. When I woke up this morning, it was just like any other day, now it's not. I feel happy. Happy that Hitler, the man who caused the war is dead. It may seem awful to feel pleased that someone has died, but when I think of Albert's wife Elsie and little Alice Stevens and all the thousands or probably millions of people who have died because of the war, I can't feel anything but happiness for his death.

Tom is so excited, asking Mother when she thinks that his Father will be home.

"We will have to listen to the radio and read what's happening in the newspapers. I think that it will take a while to return soldiers and prisoners of war back to their families if the war is over" she says.

Even though it's such a special day, we have still got to go to school. In the playground, all the children are talking about Hitlers death.

"I don't think it's true. It's a trick. He ain't dead. He's got away somewhere cos we're winning the war. He's clever, that Hitler bloke. He's got doubles to stand in for him you know" this is Joe's opinion.

"That's a load of rubbish. If its been announced on the radio, it must be true" says another boy.

Joe doesn't take too kindly to anyone who disagrees with what he says, so he immediately starts a fight with the boy. Miss Adams sees what's going on and she rushes over to break it up. Joe seems to have come off worst. His nose is bleeding and he has a scratch down his cheek. I sometimes wonder if, when Hitler was a boy, whether he was anything like Joe.

22 It's been a few days since the news flash about Hitler's death came on the radio. Headlines in the newspapers are full of it, but there hasn't been an official announcement from our Prime Minister yet. Everyone wants to know if the war is over or not. Father says it shouldn't be long now before we hear something on the radio.

Tom is still worried about his Father. This evening, we are playing with the train set on the floor in the sitting room. We have built a small bridge out of thin books for the train to run over. It took a while to get the bridge right because if the track is too steep, the train can't climb it. After swapping the books around a few times, we finally got it to work. I'm doing most of the running of the train and carriages. Tom doesn't seem to be very interested now that Mother has turned on the radio to listen to a BBC piano recital. He's hoping for news of prisoners of war.

Titch is annoying Tilly, trying to push her off the fireside mat. I think that the cats get on better with Annie than with each other. Tilly won't budge an inch and she wails and hisses loudly at Titch.

"Shush!" says Mother, turning the volume up.

Suddenly, the piano music stops and a voice says

"It is understood that in accordance with arrangements between the three great powers, an official announcement will be broadcast by the Prime Minister at

3 o'clock tomorrow afternoon, Tuesday 8th May.

In view of this fact, tomorrow, Tuesday 8th May, will be treated as Victory in Europe Day and will be regarded as a holiday. The following day, Wednesday 9th May, will also be a holiday. His Majesty the King will broadcast to the people of the British Empire and the Commonwealth, tomorrow, Tuesday 8th May at 9 pm."

"Thank goodness" says Mother.

Father gets up from his chair, goes over to where Mother is sitting, puts his arm around her shoulders and gives her a kiss. Mother has tears in her eyes as she and Father come and bend down beside Tom and me and cuddle us. Although I think that I am really getting too old for cuddles, it's rather nice when Mother kisses me on the cheek and strokes my hair.

I can't really believe that it's all over. Even though Father has been saying that we would soon hear something on the radio, when the announcement came, it was still a surprise. And, after I'd heard it, the first thing that I thought was, Alice Stevens should be here with her family hearing this. I feel so sad for Alice, whom I'd met for only just a few minutes, and I'm sure that I will never forget her or the terrible thing that happened to her.

So this is it. The end of the war in Europe. We've waited six long years for this moment. Years of never knowing from one day to the next what was going to happen to us, and I realise that because I was only five years old when the war started, I can hardly remember what life was like before there was a war.

23 The sun is shining through a gap in the curtains in my bedroom. I've been lying in bed watching the beam of light spread across the green linoleum floor.

It was very late when we all got to bed last night. Everything went crazy after the announcement on the radio. People were coming out of their houses, cheering and hugging each other and looking glad to be alive. Like us, they had survived the war. Like us, they were the lucky ones.

Mr and Mrs Thomas knocked on the front door. Mr Thomas was holding a bottle of champagne, which he said that he had been keeping all through the war for this day. We all had a glass to celebrate. It's the first time that I have had champagne. It's not as nice as fizzy lemonade.

Tom and I got kissed and cuddled all over again by Mrs Thomas. She's so pleased because Frank has got in touch with them to let them know that he should be home very soon.

I notice that Tom's bed is empty. Putting on my dressing gown and slippers, I go over to the window and draw back the curtains, letting the sunlight flood into the room. There isn't a cloud in the sky and it's quite warm. I think that the weather has been told that it can't possibly be anything but perfect for such a special day.

Tom and Mother are in the kitchen. There's a smell of baking.

"Good morning William" says Mother.

"Good morning Mother, good morning Tom" I reply.

Mother says "Father's gone to see if Albert would like to come and join us today. We thought that as the weather is warm, it would be nice to have a little party in the garden. Mr and Mrs Thomas will be round when Mrs Thomas has finished getting Frank's room ready for him"

Tom is picking at his breakfast. How I wish that he would hear from his Father. To have Mr Finch back safe and sound would be the best thing ever for Tom.

Mother gives me some toast and a cup of tea.

"I thought that we might decorate the garden. The shops have got lots of bunting ready for everyone, so after breakfast, we'll go and get some. You boys can put it up for me whilst I do the food"

We are walking to the shops and I say how strange it is to see people looking so happy.

"It's as if everyone's birthdays have all come at the same time" says Mother.

Some houses have already got bunting up, little flags moving gently in the warm air, and there is the sound of voices and music coming from open windows.

We've got the bunting and are back home.

"Come on Tom. Let's make the garden look nice" I say, trying to keep him busy.

Tom and I take the washing line down and tie the bunting to the two posts. Mother has found an old Union Jack flag in the loft, so we tie it to a stick and put it on top of the air raid shelter. I look at the shelter and think of all the nights that I've spent in there. Father will probably take it down soon, and I'm sure that we won't miss it. I wonder if Mother will plant some more rose bushes and get rid of the vegetable garden. I hope she keeps some space for growing vegetables. The vegetables tasted lovely, and it was those that helped to keep us fed. No one knows how long we will have to stay on food rationing now that the war is over.

We help Mother to carry the kitchen table and as many chairs as we can find around the house, into the garden. Tilly isn't interested in what is going on. She is stretched out on the path enjoying the sun, but as soon as we have put the table underneath the bunting line, Titch climbs onto it and tries to jump up to reach the little flags. Even though she is very athletic, the bunting is still too high up for her to get at, so after a while, she gives up and goes to play with the flag on the air raid shelter instead.

Tom has cheered up a bit. He sorted through the loft to see if there was anything else to use as decorations and came across a bag of balloons. He's just starting to blow them up when Father returns with Albert and Annie. Annie is wearing a red, white and blue striped ribbon round her neck and Albert is dressed in a blue suit. When Mother says how smart he looks in the suit, Albert says

"I hope it doesn't smell too much of mothballs. It's been in a box for ages, but I thought that I'd better look my best for today"

Father moves the radio into the kitchen and stands it on the windowsill so that we will be able to hear the Prime Minister's speech at 3 o' clock. It's now 1pm.

Mother has gone to change her clothes and she has told Tom and me to wash and tidy ourselves after we have finished putting the balloons up. Not all of the balloons work, the rubber has rotted on some of them and two burst while Tom was blowing them up, but we have ended up with eight of different colours to tie around the garden.

Mr and Mrs Thomas arrive carrying trays of food. There's corned beef sandwiches

(Mother made corned beef ones too, so we'll have lots of sandwiches to eat, but I'm sure that they will all go) Battenberg cake, and a pink blancmange. I love blancmange, especially the strawberry flavoured ones. Albert has some more of his endless supply of toffees and Mother made a sponge cake and rhubarb crumble so we are really having a treat today with all this lovely food.

Tom and I have had a quick wash and run a comb through our hair just to please Mother. When we come back into the garden, the radio is playing dance music. I'm surprised to see that Father and Mother are dancing to the music. Father has changed into a brown suit and Mother has a blue dress with white spots on it. They look so happy, as if they haven't a worry in the world.

"Would you care to dance young William?" says Mrs Thomas, giggling like a schoolgirl.

Before I can reply, she grabs hold of me, and pressing me against her large bosom, she whisks me around the garden. Round and round we go, nearly treading on Mother's vegetable plants in our mad dance.

Then, it's Tom's turn for the same treatment. It's really funny watching the two of them, and I must say that Mrs Thomas has plenty of energy for her age. When she isn't dancing, she is joining in with the Vera Lynn songs that have come on the radio. Mr Thomas and Albert seem content to just sit in the shade, talking and drinking cups of tea and Annie and the cats have gone to sleep.

Mother says to help ourselves to the food. I manage to eat five sandwiches, two helpings of blancmange, a slice of Battenberg cake and a piece of sponge cake. After all this, I feel a bit sick. So does Tom, who ate even more than I did!

We flop down onto an old garden hammock that Father put out after he remembered that we still had it in the shed. The movement of the hammock makes us feel even sicker, so we quickly get off it and sit on chairs instead.

"Nearly time for the Prime Minister's speech" says Mr Thomas, looking at his watch.

Father turns the radio up a bit so we can listen.

Then, there is a hush in the noise from the gardens all around us where other people are celebrating. Everyone wants to hear what the Prime Minister Winston Churchill has to say.

The speech starts

"Yesterday at 2.41 am at General Eisenhower's headquarters, General Jodl, representative of the German High Command and Admiral Doenitz, designated head of the German State, signed the act of unconditional surrender of all German land, sea and air forces in Europe to the Allied Expeditionary Force and simultaneously to the Soviet High Command.

Today, this agreement will be ratified and confirmed at Berlin. Hostilities will end officially at one minute after midnight, tonight Tuesday 8th May, but in the interests of saving lives, the "Cease Fire" began yesterday to be sounded along all fronts. The German war is therefore at an end."

The speech is followed by the National Anthem, which all the grown ups stand up for, so Tom and I do the same, until half way through, when Tom has to run indoors to be sick.

Tom and I soon recovered from our over eating, and a few hours later, felt hungry again, so we ate a few more sandwiches and some crumble.

Now, it's 8.50 pm. Mr and Mrs Thomas have gone back to their house with Frank who arrived home at half past five. He didn't stay for very long, just had a cup of tea and a piece of cake. He looked tired and was rather quiet, not jolly like I remember him as.

Mother has invited Albert to stay for the night and she has made up a bed for him in a corner of the sitting room. Mrs Thomas lent us a camp bed, which she says is quite comfortable, so this is what Albert will sleep on.

We've tidied up the garden and brought all the furniture back indoors. Tilly and Titch have burst all the balloons and both they and Annie had some corned beef for their tea.

"Dorothy, the King's speech will be starting in a few minutes" Father calls to Mother who is in the kitchen. He is putting the radio back on the sideboard and is turning it on. Mother comes into the room and sits down on the sofa next to Albert. The clock chimes 9 pm and the King speaks

"Speaking from our Empire's oldest capitol city, war battered, but never for one moment daunted or dismayed, speaking from London, I ask you to join me in the act of thanksgiving

Germany, the enemy who drove all Europe into war has finally been overcome.

There is great comfort in the thought that the years of darkness and danger in which the children of our Country have grown up, are over, and please God, forever"

The day seems to have gone so quickly, and there's not much left of it now. A day to go down in history, Father says – Victory in Europe Day, 8th May 1945.

24

"He's not the same"

Mrs Thomas's voice is coming from the kitchen where Mother is washing up after breakfast.

Father and Tom have gone with Albert to take Annie for a walk. I offered to stay behind and help Mother. I've just carried the blankets from Albert's bed back upstairs and put them in the cupboard.

I stop at the foot of the stairs, not wanting to barge in on their conversation.

"He's different, not at all like my Frank. I thought that we'd have so much to talk about, but he hardly said a word when we got home, and, do you know, he didn't want to sleep in his room last night. He went into the garden and laid his blankets on the grass and that's where I found him this morning. He says his beds not comfortable. I ask you, how can lying on the ground be better than a nice soft bed?"

"Well, I think it will take some time for men that have been soldiers to adjust to being home again. Frank's probably got so used to sleeping outside, that now home life must seem strange to him" Mother is trying to comfort Mrs Thomas.

"Stan just says, tell him to come indoors, but he's a grown man now not a little boy" Mrs Thomas sounds very upset.

"I think that it might help if you talk to Stan and try to make him understand that Frank will need plenty of time to settle back into everyday life. He's been a soldier for so long, that it must be difficult to suddenly stop being one"

"Yes, I'll have a word with him. It's so worrying though, not as I'd imagined Frank's coming home would be like"

I hear the chair scraping on the floor as Mrs Thomas pushes it under the table.

"Best be getting back now" she says.

Poor Mrs Thomas and poor Frank. I remember Miss Adams saying that war changes people, but I hope that it won't change Frank forever.

Father, Tom and Albert return from their walk with Annie. It's still lovely weather and Annie is so thirsty that she drinks half a bowl of water. Mother makes some tea and we're sitting at the table drinking it, when there is a knock on the door.

I open the door and find a man that I've never seen before standing on the doorstep. His face is worn and tired with dark circles under his eyes and his hair is short and greying.

"Excuse me, I'm Robert Finch, Tom's father. You must be William" he says

I hardly recognise this man from the man in Tom's photograph. He looks so much older. But, he's here and now Tom won't have to wait any longer for his Father.

"Yes, come in" I say, and then I yell out "TOM"

Tom rushes out of the kitchen, runs down the hall and throws himself at Mr Finch, who puts his arms around his son and holds him tight.

I go to tell Mother, Father and Albert the good news.